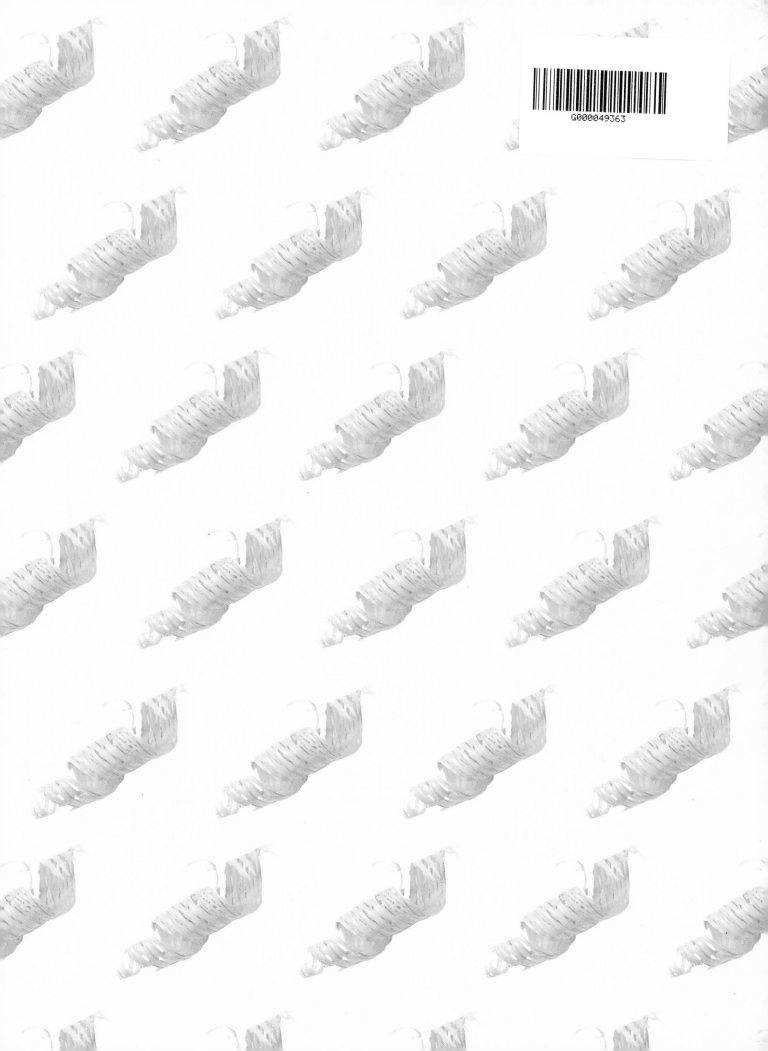

# BASIC
# WOODWORKING
# TECHNIQUES

# BASIC WOODWORKING TECHNIQUES

18 JOINERY PROJECTS
TO SHARPEN YOUR HAND AND
POWER TOOL SKILLS

DICK BURROWS

THE
APPLE
PRESS

A Quintet Book

Published by The Apple Press
6 Blundell Street
London N7 9BH

ISBN 1-85076-434-4

This book was designed and produced by
Quintet Publishing Limited
6 Blundell Street
London N7 9BH

Creative Director: Richard Dewing
Designer: Fiona Akehurst
Project Editor: Katie Preston
Editor: Geraldine Christy
Photographer: Scott Landis

Typeset in Great Britain by
The Design Revolution
Manufactured in Singapore by
Eray Scan (Pte) Limited
Printed in Singapore by
Star Standard Industries (Pte) Limited

**Publisher's Note:**
Woodworking can be dangerous.
Both hand and power tools can quickly sever
nerves, tendons, or limbs with disastrous
results. Always exercise extreme caution.
Always read the instruction manuals provided by
the manufacturers and use the safety guards
provided; for the purposes of photography, many
of the guards were removed – it is not a
recommended procedure.

As far as the methods and techniques
mentioned in this book are concerned, all
statements, information, and advice given here
are believed to be true and accurate.
However, neither the author, copyright holder,
nor the publisher can accept any legal liability
for errors or omissions.

# Contents

## Part I: Tools and Equipment

## Part II: Practical Projects

# Part 1 –
# Tools and Equipment

# 1 *Introduction*

*Wood is a beautiful, practical and adaptable medium which appeals to us all. And, whether it's a complicated inlaid box or a simple pine kitchen table, we always assume that highly skilled craftsmen created the objects we admire; it doesn't occur to us that a beginner could tackle a dovetailed box, let alone a large piece of furniture*

Woodworking is an art and a craft with a secret. It looks considerably more complex than it really is. You might assume that a cabinet, desk or other large piece would be just too difficult to build. But, in fact, the most elaborate piece of furniture is fairly simple, once you break it down into its basic components.

These components, or building blocks, can be produced with techniques that are well within the reach of any careful, determined hobbyist. Even the elegant and strong dovetail joint, which has long been considered by many woodworkers and connoisseurs to be the epitome of craftsmanship, involves very few steps. If you can lay out a line, then saw to it, you are well on your way to success.

This book is designed to present the basic techniques of woodworking needed to build simple furniture. Once you learn a little about the nature of wood, measuring, using handsaws and chisels, sharpening and basic power tools, you can begin enjoying the satisfaction that comes from mastering a craft centred upon one of the most beautiful materials on earth.

Wood has always fascinated human beings. Wood feels warm, it is easy to work, it is found in most parts of the world, it is relatively inexpensive, durable, and it can be shaped into millions of objects, from a fishing hook to a plow to a complete home. And every time you cut into a piece you will discover a landscape of patterns and colours that can intrigue the mind and delight the soul.

As you work, take every project one step at a time. And practice, practice, practice. Once you know the basics, it takes decades to become a real master of the craft. Learning to design furniture can easily take a lifetime, and there is always a new idea to try, but that is part of the fun. Without something new to learn or to do, woodworking would get boring. Even the most enthusiastic golfers would throw their clubs into the water hazard if every shot was a hole in one.

Enjoy the work and the objects you produce. You will probably discover that even your early efforts are as good as some of the work being marketed as craft today, and your customized objects will be prized by friends and family.

# 2 *Basic Equipment*

As a beginner woodworker, I eagerly pored over every new catalogue and store display I could find. I was sure that the next tool would be the one that came with the skill. My wife was more cynical. She said I had just found a way to spend money and avoid actually doing any work. She was right.

Tools are important, but working and developing skills are much more essential. Take your time, buy tools as you learn how to use them and as you need them for specific jobs. And buy good ones. A cheap, poorly designed tool will be a frustration and you will end up replacing or breaking it before long anyway.

Power tools are especially tempting, because they can do so much work quickly, but speed is not that important unless you are trying to make a living. Though I did not realize it at the time, it was good that a growing family and slim bank account prevented me from buying too many power tools right away. Hand tools encourage you to develop skill, as well as an understanding of wood, a sometimes contrary material with a mind all its own. Often the knots, fibres and other natural characteristics fight you. The only effective counter-attack is based on knowledge. It is fine to read about grain direction, but when you plane or carve a board, you will learn what the term means. Cut with the grain and things will go fairly smoothly. Cut against the grain and the tool will twist and dive, tearing or splitting the wood. You might never understand that if a power tool does everything for you.

Alan Peters, one of Britain's best contemporary woodworkers, started his apprenticeship in the workshops of Edward Barnsley, a true master of the craft who learned the trade long before power tools were in vogue. Over the years the Barnsley workshop changed, as did Peters, and things became more mechanized. Peters at first could not understand Barnsley's distrust of machines, but later he came to realize how machines can drain the life out of a piece. The best work has a joy and spontaneity, Peters says, that "is a direct result of contact with the materials at all stages with hand tools and hand skills."

Peters also counters claims that handwork is too time consuming. In his book *Cabinet Making: The Professional Approach* Peters says,

**❝ For the amateur and semi-retired professional, where time is not of any great importance, you might ask why you should spend your leisure time and retirement endangering your health by working with noisy, dusty portable routers, planers, body grinders and spray guns, for example, when hand tools are much more relaxing, even if they do demand more skill. ❞**

*Right: The Workmate is a low-cost bench for sawing and other operations, and a good portable stand for tools like router tables.*

## A place to work

Woodworking is dirty work, and often you cannot finish a job in a single day. Those who live with you might be a little upset when the television is blocked by a half-built cupboard or when all the house plants suffocate under a blanket of fine sawdust.

My first workshop was tucked into a walk-in cupboard. Workshops are commonly found in basements, spare rooms, garages, sheds and other outbuildings. I once saw a portable workshop mounted on wheels. The craftsman just rolled the unit out of the garage onto the driveway, where he had plenty of room to work.

Initially, your choice of woodworking projects will depend on your available workshop space. If you already have a workshop, you are ready to work. My workshop is a fairly simple set-up in a one-car garage. I keep my tools on pegs and open shelves, so that they are easy to find,

**Above: A sharp hand plane can efficiently flatten and polish a wood panel to create a shimmering surface that glows under a clear oil finish.**

but some woodworkers prefer to house everything in cupboards. If you do not have a workshop, invest a little time in improvising a way to work. The minimum requirements are a little space and a bench or table to support the wood while you work. If you do not have space for a permanent bench, investigate the Workmate, manufactured by Black & Decker. This well-designed bench offers several ways to clamp pieces of wood, is at a convenient height for sawing and other hand operations and can be folded up and put out of the way at the end of the day. In addition, it makes a handy platform for temporarily setting up other tools, such as a router table.

### Basic hand tools

- A bench or Workmate work station
- Saws – back saw, cross-cut, rip, coping saw
- T-square
- Tape measure
- Compass
- Soft-faced hammer or mallet
- Awl
- Nail sets
- Files, rasps, Surform scrapers
- Bevel or combination square
- Pencils
- Marking and/or morticing gauge
- Knife
- Several chisels – firmer, pairing and mortice
- Sharpening tools

# 3 *Basic Power Tools*

As you can imagine, I did not fit many power tools into my first workshop. Initially I had the timberyard rough cut the stock and surface it. Milled wood is generally more expensive than rough stock, but at least you can start building with a minimum of fuss and mess. Later I enrolled in an adult education class. One night a week I went to the local high school workshop and used their machines. I built my first workbench there, and learned the basics of using power tools at the same time. And regardless of what I was building in class, I would bring a couple of extra boards to run through the planer, so I would have plenty of wood to work on at home.

Another option is to rough out the stock by hand, with planes, saws and chisels. Before the age of power, generations of woodworkers did that. But it is a great deal of work, and perhaps more of an aerobic workout than most people like. Ripping a 2.4m (8ft) boat in half with a hand saw

*Left: A medium–powered electric drill is an essential woodworking tool. Although most people buy a drill powered by mains electricity (bottom), cordless drills (top) are quieter, lighter, and there is no extension cord to worry about*

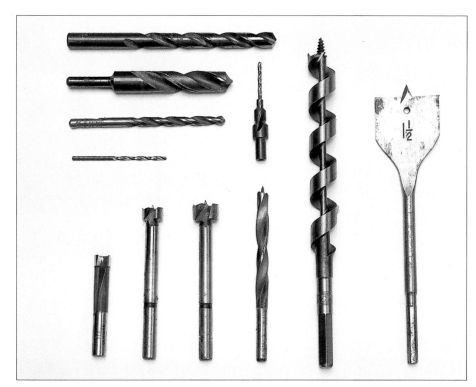

can be tedious. Flattening the sawn board with hand planes is also very demanding, but it is a good skill to learn, and will teach you much about the nature of wood. Some day, unless you have oversized industrial tools, you are going to have to hand plane a table top or other broad surface, so you might as well start learning and acquire the skill for all your work.

If you have the money, invest in some power tools. Start with an electric-powered hand drill. The variable speed models offer the most versatility. You can start a hole at low speed, then increase the rpm to suit the material once you have everything aligned. Standard twist bits for metal, like the ones shown in the top left corner, are fine for drilling small holes in wood; paddle-shaped spade bits, like the 38 mm (1½ in) bit shown on the far right, are for larger holes. The other bits shown are, from right to left, a power auger bit, which like the spade bit is good for boring large holes in wood; to the left of the auger bit is a brad point bit or "dowel bit", which has a centre point to help start a hole accurately and prevent the bit from skipping across the surface of the wood. Above the brad point is a bit designed to drill a lead hole for a screw and expand the top of the opening in one operation. These bits let you install screws below the surface of the wood, an operation called countersinking. The three bits in the lower left corner are Forstner bits, designed to bore flat bottom holes. Since these bits do not have lead screws, like auger bits, to

help pull them into the wood, they work best in a drill press.

Bits are usually available in either tungsten carbide or high-speed steel. The tungsten carbide bits stay sharper longer than high-speed steel, especially for cutting manmade materials such as plywood or chipboard.

A **router** is a real boon to a woodworker with a modest workshop. It can do a wide variety of shaping and cutting tasks. It is noisy and must be treated with respect, as any tool must, but it is a very versatile item. Long ago, a friend told me that a router would mean an instant improvement in my work. I did not believe him at first, but once I got one and realized how quickly and precisely it could shape the edges of tables and benches, I realized he was right. A single router, equipped with bits like those shown, can replace a wall full of specialized planes for cutting joints and shaping pieces of wood.

*Above: Modern bits make a power drill a versatile workhorse in any shop. On the left, from top to bottom, are three standard twist bits. The bits below, from left to right, are three Forstner bits, a "brad" point bit, an auger bit and a 38 mm (1½ in.) spade bit.*

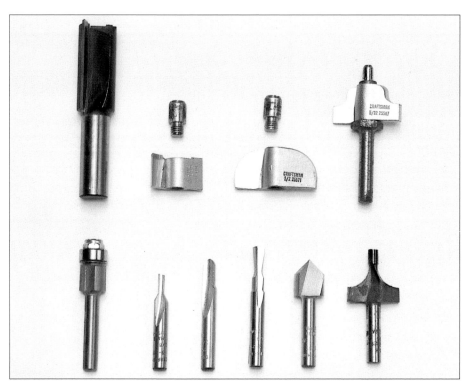

Despite its versatility, the router is not an instant cure-all. It is powerful, fast and can be dangerously difficult to control. Before you begin using one, check out the owner's manual on jigs and bit types to help control the machine. My sister-in-law built a nice little coffee table, then decided to round over the edges of the top. Her instructor gave her a router and advised her to get on with it. She botched the job and turned the straight edge into a maze of humps and valleys. Later she found out that she should have used a fence to guide the machine or a bit with a built-in control bearing. Like many other powerful tools, a router is not designed to be used freehand.

Sanding is an essential task, but it can be a real chore to do a large object with a piece of sandpaper wrapped around a block of wood. Modern **pad** or **orbital sanders**, which use a quarter or half sheet of sandpaper, are a joy. They are relatively quiet, easy to use and can be equipped with dust bags to help eliminate the dust clouds that sanders are capable of producing. Newer models use adhesive or Velcro-backed papers, which are quick to fasten tightly to the sanding pad and work much more effectively than loose sheets of sandpaper held on the pad with some type of clip.

*The bits shown are, top row (left to right): a 13-mm ($\frac{1}{2}$-in) diameter carbide straight bit, and three high-speed steel cutters, with guide bearings. They are designed to cut rebates, coves and ogee shapes. The cutters are mounted on a shank, like the one shown at right. By changing the guide bearings on top of the shank, you can adjust the distance between the cutting edge and the fence used to guide the bit. The bottom row includes a flush trimming bit, with a guide bearing that is exactly the same diameter as the cutter itself. This bit is very handy for trimming overhanging veneer or plastic laminate flush with the edge of a counter top. The next four bits are for cutting various shaped grooves. The last bit is a one-piece bit with an attached guide bearing.*

*Right: A plunge router, guided by a simple wood fence, can cut an accurate mortice much faster than traditional hand methods.*

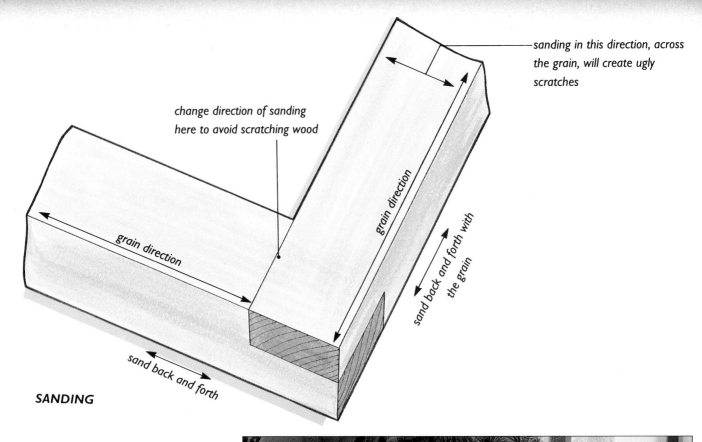

sanding in this direction, across the grain, will create ugly scratches

change direction of sanding here to avoid scratching wood

grain direction

grain direction

sand back and forth with the grain

sand back and forth

**SANDING**

*Right: Not many woodworkers enjoy sanding, but small, powerful orbital sanders eliminate much of the tedium of this essential job.*

## FINISHING WITH A BELT SANDER

Belt sanders are so efficient at removing wood that some woodworkers call them "abrasive planers". They are very useful when you have a great deal of sanding to do, especially if the job includes a broad surface, such as a table top. But they can be hard to control.

The typical portable belt sander drives a circular abrasive belt that is 75–100 mm (3–4 in) wide and 460–600 mm (18–24 in) in circumference. The belt runs on two rollers. One is powered by an electric motor; the other is free running, but can be angled to keep the belt running true on the rollers. Between the two rollers, on the bottom of the sander, is a flat metal plate, called a platten, that holds the moving belt flat down on the surface being sanded.

Because of the speed at which the belt travels, never stop moving the sander as long as the belt is running. If you do, you are liable to gouge the wood. If you are sanding a veneered piece, you can cut all the way through the thin layer of wood in a heartbeat if you are careless. The danger is especially great on corners and edges, fragile sections that can be obliterated by the power of the sander.

As with any hand or machine sanding, also be careful always to sand with the grain, as shown in the drawing.

Always start sanding with coarse grits and work progressively toward finer grits.

## UNDERSTANDING SANDPAPER GRITS

Sandpaper is available in a variety of grits, generally from 36 grit up to grits in the 1,000s for fine finishing papers used by car-body repairers. The lower the number, the coarser the paper – 36 grit paper, for example, is so rough it feels like pebbles glued on to heavy paper.

If you work carefully while building the piece, you should not have to start sanding with anything coarser than 100 grit. If possible, you might want to do some of this initial sanding before you assemble the piece. Components are always easier to sand when they can be spread out on a bench.

When you have everything smooth and clean with 100 grit, move to 120, then 150 and then to 180 and 220. Each finer grit of paper

reduces the scratches left by the previous, coarser grade. You can see these scratches if you look across the wood surface at a low angle. Shining a light across the wood helps pick the scratches up.

Generally, you must sand to 220 before you can apply a finish. Scratches left by coarser paper often look like jagged canyons when oil or another finish is applied.

It is always tempting to skip grits and get right to the fine paper, but I have always found it just makes the job harder and more tiresome.

**1 Flexible sandpaper**

**2 Flour paper**

**3 Self-lubricating silicon carbide paper**

**4 Glasspaper**

**5 Fine garnet paper**

**6 Coarse garnet paper**

**7 Coarse aluminium oxide paper**

# 4 *Stationary Power Tools*

So far, I have not mentioned any of the big tools that are the pride of many amateurs and an essential part of the professional's efforts to make a living. If you have visited an established workshop, you will have seen table-saws and bandsaws for cutting wood, planers for flattening boards and cutting to thickness, and overhand planers to square up the edges of components, along with a variety of sanders that can reduce wood to dust in seconds.

These tools offer several advantages. They significantly reduce the drudgery of woodworking, offer accuracy and versatility, and make it possible to tackle any project quickly and efficiently. On the down side, they are very expensive, require a fair bit of maintenance and adjustment, can be very dangerous and put out high levels of noise and air pollution.

If you have access to these machines, by all means learn to use them. Get professional training if possible. If you do not have access to any educational courses, perhaps the agent or an experienced woodworker in your area could help. Otherwise, the manufacturers offer manuals, and often videos, to get you started. Just remember to be very careful and observe all safety precautions. A friend of mine always says, "Before you turn on any power tool, turn on your concentration."

If you decide to buy your own power tools, talk with as many dealers and experienced woodworkers as you can, before you get out the cheque book. Make sure the tools you are considering are suited to the work you do and your workshop. You do not want a tool that you will quickly outgrow, but you also do not want one that is so powerful that you do not have the skill to operate it safely.

There is also a fair amount of debate among woodworkers about which power tool to buy first. Some recommend a **radial-arm saw,** because of its versatility. In addition to excelling at cross-cutting boards to length, the radial-arm saw can handle a variety of accessories for shaping and moulding wood, although I always find it awkward to use the saw to rip wide boards into narrower strips.

Others consider the **table-saw** the workhorse of the workshop, because it is ideal for ripping boards to width and cutting joints. Both the table-saw and radial-arm saw are considered too dangerous by some, who opt for a bandsaw. A large **bandsaw** can be equipped with different width belts that make it ideal for cross-cutting, ripping and joinery. Plus it makes quick work of cutting curves and odd shapes.

*Left: A table-saw is often the centre of workshop activity for shaping, grooving, mitring and jointing.*

## SAFETY

# A WORD ABOUT SAFETY GUARDS

Woodworking has many traditions, but one that must be eliminated is the three-fingered handshake. In earlier times, many woodworkers carried the mark of power-tool damage as a sign of their years working at the trade. Nowadays manufacturers, government departments and other groups have been working long to prevent that kind of accident.

Most modern power tools are now equipped with a variety of guards to help protect the operator. Do not ignore them. Use them as much as possible. (Note: Many of the guards were removed for photographic purposes in this book. It is not a recommended procedure.) If you find a guard difficult to use, do not just take it off and run unprotected. Ring the manufacturer's customer service representative to see if additional help is available. Perhaps you have not installed the guard properly or it is defective.

If you still do not like the guard, check out the various after-market devices. You will see several models demonstrated at most tool shows.

Do not work unprotected. Guards and other safety devices will never replace care and common sense, but they can be very valuable. One of the most definite laws in woodworking is that something can always go wrong.

---

The table-saw is the central item of my workshop, and so I have used it extensively in this book for both ripping and cross-cutting, as well as joinery. If the table-saw does not seem suited for cutting a certain joint, I will generally switch to a portable router and hand tools. We shall discuss basic techniques for the table-saw and overhand planer after we talk a little about wood and hand tools.

The **overhand planer** may seem like a luxury, but it is a pretty important piece of equipment. As we will see when we begin to mark out joints, you always need to begin with one straight and square reference surface. The overhand planer is made for this job. It has a large flat surface, comprised of two separate tables which can be adjusted in relation to each other to regulate the depth of cut. A sturdy fence mounted to the machine lets you run a board on edge over the tables and across the rotating knife assembly, called a cutter head, to mill the edge straight and perpendicular to the face of the board riding against the fence. You can do this job with hand planes, but it is more difficult. You can also make jigs and fixtures for your table-saw or radial-arm saw that will enable you to duplicate most of the functions of the overhand planer, although not its speed.

At present the table-saw is probably the power tool I use the most, but the bandsaw runs a close second. Mostly I use both tools to rough out stock, then do my joinery with hand tools or a portable router.

*Above: Many woodworkers prefer to use the relatively safe bandsaw – the thrust of the blade is downwards, and so there is less kickback.*

# 5 *The Nature of Wood*

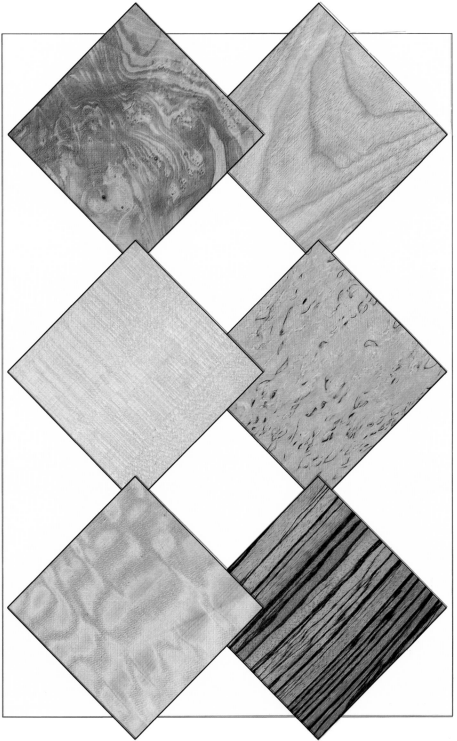

Wood, straight from the sawmill, is often so rough and dirty that many people cannot even guess what species or colour it is. Those wonderful grain patterns you see on furniture in the dealer's showroom are there, but they are hidden under rough torn fibres, grime and saw marks. The boards are also not likely to be flat either, because they will have twisted and cupped as they dried out after the tree was sawn up.

Remember, wood is a living thing. When a tree is cut down, the wood tissue is full of moisture, a stage woodworkers call green or wet. The tree is technically dead, but the wood does not become inert, like stone. It will always continue to expand, contract, twist or move in some way in response to changes in the moisture levels of the air that surrounds it.

As soon as a tree is cut, the sap and water that the tree absorbed from the ground begins to dissipate into the air. This moisture loss, especially if it is very rapid, creates stresses in the wood, which cause sections to warp, cup or form defects like cracks. In addition, areas where branches grew or where the tree might have been injured during its lifetime create other defects, which add to the problems, and sometimes the beauty of working with wood.

No matter how long it has been since the tree was cut, the wood never becomes completely dry, not even after it has been made into furniture. In dry months, especially in homes

Olive ash stumpwood (top left), flat-cut Japanese ash (top right), rippled sycamore (centre left), disease-flecked masur birch (centre right), quilted Japanese horse chestnut (bottom left), dark-striped zebrano (bottom right).

where central heating lowers humidity levels during the winter season, moisture will leave the wood and pass into the surrounding room. In damper weather, the wood will suck up moisture from the air. This exchange of moisture affects the wood enough to change the size of a board. The wood expands as it absorbs water and shrinks as it loses it.

This constant movement would be difficult enough to deal with if it happened equally in every direction, but it does not. Wood essentially moves only along its width, not along its length. Wood cells are arranged in long chains that run up and down the height of the tree. These cells do not become taller when swollen, but they do become thicker, in the same way that human beings who overeat gain in the waistline, not in height.

This difference in movement creates real problems for woodworkers when they join pieces of wood together. When you fasten a long-grain piece across the grain of a second piece, you restrict the movement of the wood, just as you would if you fastened a piece of steel across the board. When the environmental moisture level changes, the wood responds by expanding or contracting. If it is prevented from moving by some type of cross-grain construction, the wood will twist or crack, with enough force to open a joint at the corner of a door frame or to split a table top.

You can minimize problems with wood movement by avoiding cross-grain constructions and by purchasing wood that has been carefully dried. Drying the wood to a workable level of moisture is a fairly exact science.

Cabinetmakers prefer to work with wood that has moisture levels of between 8 and 12 per cent. Discuss this with a local timber merchant; he will know about working conditions in your area. Many woodworkers bring their wood into the workshop a couple of weeks before they need it, so it can adjust to the new environment before it is processed, and they design joints not to restrict wood movement. The finish applied to a piece of furniture slows down the moisture transfer somewhat, but it never eliminates it completely. To get maximum benefit from the finish, it's usually necessary to do both sides of the board. If you paint one side and leave the other side natural, you are likely to encounter problems. One exception is the insides of chests and drawers. Apparently the moisture changes inside the case are not drastic enough to cause problems, but carpenters know enough to fit drawers somewhat loosely. I was taught to leave about 2 mm ($\frac{1}{16}$ in) clearance around the drawer during the damp months and about 3 mm ($\frac{1}{8}$ in) in drier seasons, to accommodate seasonal wood movement.

*Above: A blanket chest by Luke Hughes showing the distinctive curvilinear grain of elm.*

## Selecting wood for projects

The woods of the world provide woodworkers with an astounding palette of colours, textures and grain patterns. Fortunately many of the best woods for making furniture and other woodworking projects are readily available and relatively inexpensive.

Before you head for the local timber merchant, you do need to be familiar with a few commonly used terms. The first ones you're likely to encounter are **hardwood** and **softwood**. The woods I used for the projects in this book include a variety of softwoods, like pine, and hardwoods such as oak and butternut. Softwoods come from conifers; hardwoods come from deciduous trees. Despite the "hard" and "soft" nomenclature, not all softwoods are especially soft and not all hardwoods are harder than so-called "softwoods". Poplar, for example, is a hardwood but is generally softer than the softwood pine.

Air-dried or kiln-dried woods are also common. Air-dried timber is stacked undercover, with stickers or thin slats between the layers and allowed to dry for months or years until the moisture in the wood is in equilibrium with the moisture levels in the surrounding area. Kiln-dried wood is processed in a large, wood drying oven, which reduces the moisture in the wood to about 8 to 10 per cent. Whether the wood is air-dried or kiln-dried, its moisture level will continue to adjust to environmental changes. That's why it's always a good idea to stack timber in your workshop for several weeks or months before it's needed, so it can stabilize in your environment.

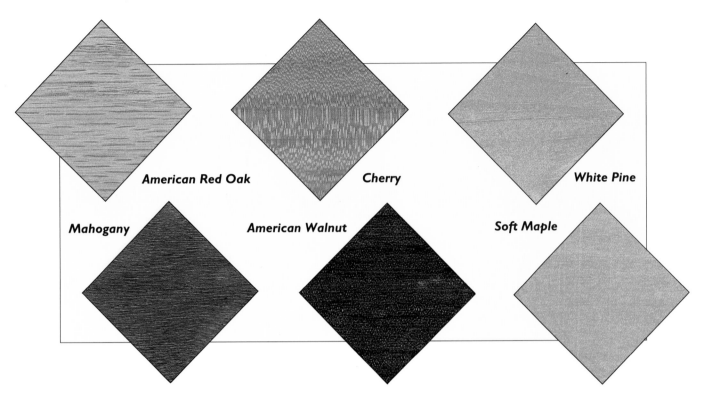

American Red Oak    Cherry    White Pine

Mahogany    American Walnut    Soft Maple

Wood can be purchased rough, planed/planed on two sides, or planed on two faces and two edges. Terms vary from country to country or even region to region, so check with your timber mercant. Hardwoods in the United Kingdom are mostly sold rough in random metric widths and lengths; softwoods are sold planed to final metric width and thickness. Wood planed to final width and thickness is generally more expensive than rough stock, because of the cost of processing the wood.

Wood may also be ordered: from clear stock, free from visible defects and FAS (first and seconds) to utility grades with many defects. Generally, the higher the grade, the fewer the defects and the higher the price. Lower grades are often very attractive, but you may waste considerable stock cutting out defects such as splits, knots and stains.

In working out how much wood you need for a project, you should also know that wood planed on all four sides is sold by nominal measure. This term describes the size of the board before it is machined, losing about 5 mm (³⁄₁₆ in) all round. You should also order 20 to 25 per cent more wood than you think you'll need to accommodate losses to defects, saw cuts and other factors.

The choice of wood depends on personal taste and the type of project you have in mind. Pine and other softwoods are most often used as construction material, but some pines make very attractive pieces. **White pine** has a light brown heartwood, which darkens as it ages, and it's easy to work with either hand or machine tools. **Mahogany** is a wonderful furniture wood, a joy to work with and it takes a fine finish. **Cherry**, one of my favourites, has a light to reddish

brown heartwood, which becomes even richer as it ages. It has attractive grain patterns and finishes well. **Black walnut** also has beautiful figures, is easy to work with and finishes well. Its heartwood is generally light to dark brown, with a nearly white sapwood. **Oak** is very strong and quite popular now for contemporary furniture. **Maple**, because of its durability and light colour, is a favourite for many furniture pieces, as well as household objects such as bowls and cutting boards. Sugar maple often displays flamboyant figures such as bird's eye, fiddle back or curly grain patterns, but can be difficult to work.

## Working with Plywood

Plywood can be both a blessing and a curse. It seems a logical material to choose whenever you need a flat, broad surface, and in many cases it is, but you do have to take special precautions to get the best results from the material.

You also have to take special measures to handle it. A "four-by-eight" sheet of plywood is very heavy, hard to handle and maneuver in a shop and can be a real problem to cut on an average-sized table. A helper is always a good idea, I find, when working with plywood.

Plywood comes in many grades. Basically it is a glue and wood sandwich assembled by laminating several layers of thinly sliced wood together. The best grades have more layers, called plies, and the layers are likely to be a better wood than those in the lower grades. These lower grades are also likely to contain more voids – open areas in the lamination – than the better grades.

Top-quality plywood will have face veneers that are as beautiful as any piece of solid wood. You can buy maple, cherry, walnut and other very spectacular species. Many exotics, which are not available in large, solid wood chunks, can be obtained as veneer and these can be applied to plywood or other manmade materials, such as chipboard or Medium Density Fibreboard (MDF), for exquisite effects.

The real advantage of plywood and other similar materials is that they are dimensionally stable. Plywood does not expand and contract in the way that solid wood does, so it can be used

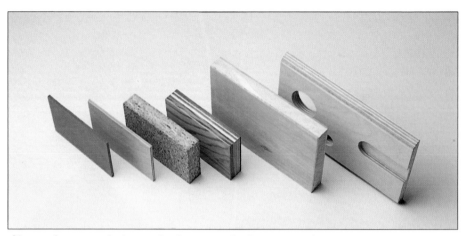

*Above: A range of plywood of varying thicknesses and quality, including three-ply and decorative.*

on broad surfaces. The material can warp or bend, however, so it is necessary to make sure that it is adequately framed and supported.

An unattractive part of the plywood can be removed by one of these supporting systems, called lipping; a thin strip of solid wood is applied around the edges of the plywood to make the sheet appear to be a solid piece of wood. In the process the strip hides the edges of the sheet, where the laminations and glue lines are visible. Most people find these end views unattractive.

Plywood can be machined with the same tools as solid wood, but it tends to dull tools faster because of the hardness of the glue lines. If you ignore warnings about planing an edge of a plywood sheet, for example, you will most likely make a mess of the edge and the glue will nick out sections of your planer knives, forcing you to have the blades resharpened.

Most of the joints favoured for solid wood are not nearly as effective in plywood because of the ply structure.

Splined mitres are good, though, as are standard biscuit joint and dowel set-ups.

Surface veneers are also somewhat more prone to tearing out than solid wood. When sawing, put the show face of the plywood toward the cutting edge of the teeth. That way the teeth strike the surface and cut it first, while it is supported by the body of the sheet. This makes the show surface less likely to tear than the bottom surface of the plywood. Some workers cover the cut lines with masking tape to reinforce the fibres. Also make sure that the throat plate on your saw is snug to the blade, to minimize tearing.

Most finishes that work for solid wood are also effective with plywood. In preparing the surface remember that the top layer is not as thick as the whole sheet. Over-aggressive sanding on the surfaces, especially near the edges, can create ugly spots that are nearly impossible to hide. As with solid wood, make sure to finish both sides of the plywood, to protect the wood from moisture and grime.

# 6 *Thoughts on Design*

It is not usually practical to carve furniture out of solid wood. It would be very laborious to carve a chair out of a tree, for example, because you would have to start with such a large chunk of wood and the waste would be excessive. Also, such a large block would present major wood movement problems and many sections would not be strong enough.

Remember, chains of wood fibres are arranged up and down the trunk of the tree. Wood is very strong when these fibres are intact, but if you slice the fibres into thin strips, the cross-grain is very weak. This is much like what happens when you slice a steak into thin strips across the grain. There are no long strong fibres to reinforce the piece. The material holding the little segments of the chain side by side are not nearly as strong as the long chains themselves. You can see how a thin slice snaps like a cracker, while a long-grain strip can be bent into a significant curve.

Cabinetmakers get away from the natural weaknesses of wood and make maximum use of the material by joining smaller pieces of wood together. The art of hooking these pieces together in a strong, functional and attractive way is called joinery. We shall be making several of these joints later in the book.

Furniture design, of course, goes beyond considerations of joinery. "Furniture must be designed so that people will use it, so that it will withstand hard use, and so that it pleases the eye," says David Field, a

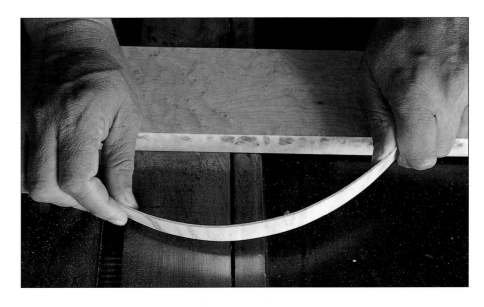

*Right: Wood is very strong and flexible along its grain (top) because of the way fibres run up and down the tree, but a slice breaks easily across the grain (right).*

faculty member at the Royal College of Art in London. He identifies three elements of design: use, ease and economy and beauty. The interplay of these items can be very subtle, and often depends largely on an individual's personal taste and preferences.

That sounds pretty intimidating, doesn't it? I know the first response

from many woodworkers is that they claim they cannot design. Many spend their whole time working with plans drawn up by somebody else. This is fine, of course, and often quite a challenge, especially when you reproduce classic museum pieces. The workmanship and attention to details on many of these classics is exquisite. Trying to duplicate the

# WHAT IS ORIGINALITY?

Imitation is said to be the supreme form of flattery, but when it comes to copying another person's furniture designs, some call that stealing, especially if you are building the piece for resale.

This cannot possibly be stealing, others say, because there is nothing new under the sun and the person who drew up the plans probably lifted the idea from somewhere else anyway. I must admit that in the beginning I felt that working as hard as I had to master the techniques of woodworking gave me a license to reproduce anything I had the skill to build.

Most woodworkers I know do not really object if someone builds one of their designs for personal use. Many even write articles and provide plans for publication in various periodicals and books in the expectation that people are going to duplicate their work. They do not expect to see exact copies of their design being sold at every craft show in the county, though.

Learn from your teachers, whether it be in a full-time course or brief seminar or a magazine or book, but have enough respect for yourself and their work to move beyond what they show you. Re-interpret their ideas, change the propositions to suit your own sense of balance and beauty. Experiment with different joinery and woods. Make each piece reflect your own self.

Work out your designs on paper before starting to build. I like to use graph paper with 6 mm (¼ in) squares at this stage, because the squares help me to judge proportions and relate the various parts to each other. If the piece is complicated, draw it out full size on large sheets of paper for a more realistic test of proportions and relationships. This building-with-a-pencil stage might seem like a waste of time or an unnecessary step, but it will make the work go easier later. Professionals often work this way. Many even take the process further and build a scale model or a full-sized mock-up out of scrap wood to test their designs.

carving, joinery and finish of these masterworks can be a very demanding and rewarding part of your apprenticeship.

However, you might not be satisfied with duplicating the work of others. You might also not like all aspects of the piece depicted in the plans you buy. Perhaps you would rather make a tapered leg than a turned one. Or you would prefer three small drawers in your desk front, rather than one wide one. Perhaps your spouse collects something that just does not go with any of the display cases on the market and you need a specially built one.

Get out your pencil, a pad of paper, a ruler, maybe a calculator and give it a try. Start by adapting a picture of a piece you like. I just mount a portable drafting table on my workbench and make the design thinking a regular part of my workshop routine. Just remember design is a natural thing. Every time you rearrange the furniture in your living room or decide which tie goes with which suit and which socks, you are actually working out a design of sorts. You are arranging a group of elements in a particular situation to produce something that works for you, and at the same time appeals to your sense of what looks right, or even beautiful.

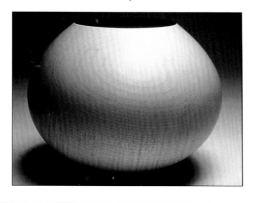

# WORKING FROM PHOTOGRAPHS

When you cannot find plans for a piece that interests you or just want to start out on your own, you might first look at a catalogue or collection of photos of furniture to help you refine your ideas. Better still, visit a museum to view good pieces for first-hand inspiration.

As long as you know at least one dimension of the pieces in a photograph you can work out the remaining dimensions without much trouble, unless you insist on making an exact duplicate.

If you are just re-interpreting the piece, though, pinpoint accuracy is not essential. To work out dimensions, I rely on a "Proportion Scale" available from artist's and draughtsman's suppliers.

This imperial scale consists of two plastic circles, each with a scale around its circumference. Both circles are pinned together at their centre points. Here is how to make it work. If you know the height of a piece is $16\frac{3}{4}$ in and measured 4 in in the photograph, match $16\frac{3}{4}$ on the outer circle with 4 on the inner. Next measure the width of the piece in the picture. Say it is 6 in. Look at 6 on the inner scale, the same scale you used for the first photo measurement. Next, read off the measurement on the outer scale to determine the actual width — 25 in this case. The process is pretty accurate, if you do not move

the scales once you start measuring photo components and scaling the measurements up to actual size.

Once you have all the rough dimensions worked out, start on your drawing. Be aware that you will have to compensate for changes in perspective and other distortions created in the photographic process. Usually I just adjust everything to suit my eye, then incorporate any new features or modifications that I think will improve the piece. All that remains is to work out the joinery and build the piece.

# 7 *Fastenings For Wood*

If joinery does such a good job of hooking pieces of wood together, why would anyone need fasteners. In the carpentry trade fasteners play a very important part in assembling strong structures, but this role is not as great in furniture making. Nails and screws do help to reinforce many joints, however, serve as aids for alignment and as holding devices to secure components. Screws are also needed for hinges and other hardware, but they are seldom necessary for reinforcing glued joints. Modern glues, such as the yellowish aliphatic resin glues marketed as wood-worker's or carpenter's glue, are much stronger than wood. When there is a break in the area of a glue joint, you will almost always find that it is the wood itself which has broken, not the glue that has come unstuck.

Cabinetmakers mostly rely on smaller wire nails, called brads, and narrow-diameter finishing nails. These are helpful in reinforcing simple butt joints or mitres and in holding pieces together while glue is drying. Because of their small diameters, they can also be sunk beneath the surface of the wood with nail sets, tapered metal punches, and hidden with wood putty or tiny wood plugs. One traditional joint is also based on a type of fastener. Dowels are narrow-diameter hardwood pegs glued into mating holes bored into the components of the joint. Dowel joints are fairly strong, and relatively easy to reglue together if they ever loosen. Some woodworkers feel they are not nearly as strong as some other joints, such as the mortice and tenon, but I have found them to be very effective, and the dowel joint is one of the easiest for beginners to master.

Typical driving instruments for fasteners and other objects in the workshop include a dead-blow hammer, a plastic-faced hammer with a special energy-absorbing head that prevents the tool from bouncing back when it hits something; a carver's mallet with a round head that makes good contact with a chisel handle no matter how it strikes the tool; a common 450 g (1 lb) carpenter's claw hammer for driving nails; and a Japanese hammer for driving fasteners and iron-hooped chisels.

*Left: Woodworkers often use dowels, the wooden pegs shown at top left, finishing nails or brads to hold components together. The black tapered punches between the nails and dowels are nail sets, which are needed to push nail heads below the surface of wood. Hammers shown are, clockwise from lower left: a dead-blow hammer, a Japanese-style hammer, carpenter's claw hammer, and wood carver's mallet.*

# 8 *A Primer on Hand Tool Use*

## *Marking out*

The two most frequently used tools in my shop are among the simplest ones I own – the square, often called a T-square, and the marking gauge. Both tools come in a variety of sizes and prices, but my favourites are fairly ordinary, the kind you can get at almost any hardware shop.

The square is simply a thin piece of metal, called a tongue, mounted in a thicker base, called the body. The pieces meet at an exact 90-degree angle, so the square offers a no-fuss way to draw a line across a board that is perfectly perpendicular to the edge. This 90-degree angle is the basis of most of the joinery work you will do.

The square is easy to use. Mark a point on the top edge of the board, put your sharp pencil point on your mark and move the square to the point. Make sure the body of the square is tight against the edge of the board and draw your line. You can draw the line along either the outside of the tongue or along the inside edge between the blade and the body. The inside edge is usually more accurate.

*Right: A T-square is indispensable in the workshop. Common uses include drawing an accurate line perpendicular to an edge of a board and drawing a straight line along an edge (bottom).*

You can buy a square with the tongue and body permanently fixed together, but I prefer an adjustable combination square, which can be set at both 90 degrees and 45 degrees. It has a metal body with a thumb screw to secure or release the blade. This enables you to adjust the length of the tongue for various applications. For example, I frequently set the tongue at a certain length, then hold the body against the edge of the board and use the end of the tongue as a guide for drawing a straight line along the edge of the board. You can also remove the tongue from the body and remount it so that it meets the body at a 45-degree angle. This is especially handy when doing mitres, which we will discuss later.

A sharp pencil is adequate for most marking-out jobs, but some workers prefer to use a knife or awl. The knife cut is finer than most pencil marks, and does not noticeably widen in the way a pencil point does as it dulls. Also, the knife will score the wood fibres, creating a little gully that provides a good reference point for starting a saw or chisel cut.

You can buy a marking knife, which is like an ordinary knife except that it has a bevel on only one side of the blade. You run the flat side of the blade against the square, then the bevel helps push the knife tight against the square as you score the line. I usually use the small blade on my Swiss Army pocket knife.

When using a square or marking gauge, make your measurements from the same edge or face of the board, which is designated as a reference surface.

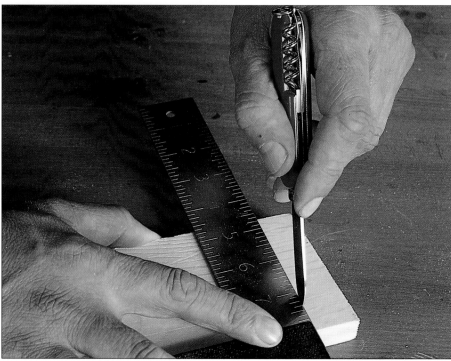

**Top: A T-square can be used to mark out a 45-degree mitre.**
**Bottom: A sharp pocket-knife, like a Swiss Army knife, can be run along the tongue of a T-square to scribe a line.**

By making all your measurements from the same surface you will have the best chance of getting the parts you need to the proper size and to have mating pieces fit.

I have two types of marking gauges in my workshop. One represents the simplest kind of gauge. Basically, it is a 150 mm (6 in) long arm, called a beam, with a small metal point protruding from it. The beam slides through a hole chopped through a block of wood, called the fence. A wedge or thumb screw in the fence locks the beam in place after you have set the distance between the point and the body of the gauge.

You can use the gauge to mark a line across the face of a board, along its length or across the end grain. Simply set the distance between the point and the fence, secure the beam, set the fence against the reference surface and pull the gauge toward you. It is better to make several light passes, rather than a single heavy pass, especially when cutting with the grain, where the point might tend to wander along the wood fibres.

The mortice gauge is very similar to a marking gauge, but the beam is equipped with two adjustable points. By setting the points to a certain width and at a certain distance from the fence you can draw both lines needed to chop a mortice or cut a tenon. The lines are very clear and easy to follow and help ensure the mortice and tenon will fit exactly. Again, make sure you draw the lines on the tenon component and the mortice component from the same reference edge.

**Top: Using a simple marking gauge to scribe a line parallel to an edge. Bottom: A mortice gauge has two cutters to mark out both sides of the mortice in a single operation.**

# JIGS, FIXTURES AND OTHER GUIDES TO ACCURACY

When I visit a museum or historic property that has preserved an eighteenth-century workshop, I am always amazed by the number of patterns, jigs and other paraphernalia that is hung around the workshop. I had always pictured the Shaker woodworkers and others as masters of eye-hand coordination and the straight line, well cut even with a hand-saw or chisel. But they were practical craftsmen. Why redo a pattern by eye or from a flimsy paper tracing when you could make one out of wood and metal and use it for years? Why risk cutting a piece wrongly when you could clamp a guide block in place to ensure the accuracy of a saw? If you work with certain angles all the time, why not make guide blocks that can be used every time?

Experiment with the ways of getting the most out of simple tools. To divide a board into equal strips, for example, place a ruler *diagonally* across the width of a piece with 0 at one end and 6 on the other. Dividing 6 into three parts equals 2, so mark off in 50 mm (2 in) increments.

You can divide a board with a compass and ruler. Use the ruler to gauge how big each part should be, set the compass to that measurement and step off the distance with the points of the compass. If the space is not

*Top: Use a ruler to estimate the size of the section.*

divided evenly, expand or close the compass as needed and step off the distance again. Refine your measurements until everything comes out evenly. A compass is also very handy for laying out circles, curves and scallop shapes on many pieces.

Learn to think about the job on hand and come up with your own guides to help you work efficiently.

*Right: Mark off equal steps with the compass.*

# Saws

Hand saws are very effective tools, especially if you are only removing the small amount of material needed to create most joints. It is important that they are sharp. I find I do not have the patience or the eyesight to do a good job of sharpening saws, so I let the guys at the tool centre do it.

Common workshop saws include a carpenter's saw, either rip or cross-cut; a Japanese Ryobi saw which has rip teeth on one edge and cross-cut on the other; a backsaw for cutting tenons and other joint components and a thin-blade, fine-toothed saw for cutting dovetail joints.

Cross-cut saws are designed to cut across the grain. Generally they have 8 to 10 teeth per 25 mm (1 in), referred to as points, and cut across a board fairly smoothly without tearing the wood. Rip saws cut with the grain, which is much more difficult to do than cross-cut, so they generally have only 4 to 6 points per 25 mm (1 in) and make a more aggressive cut. Even though the rip saw is designed to handle long-grain cuts, a 2.4m (8 ft) board will seem endless by the third time you try to rip a narrow strip off it.

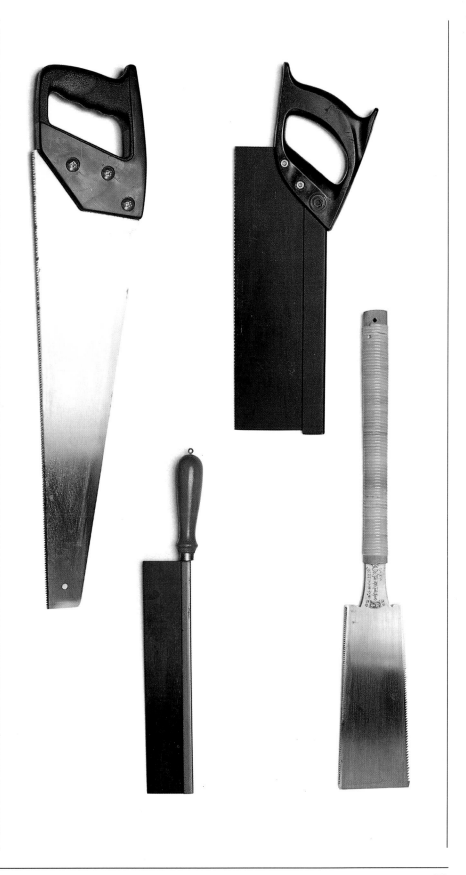

*Right: Saws come in many sizes and shapes. Clockwise from top left: carpenter's cross-cut saw, a back saw for cutting tenons and other joinery, a thin Japanese saw with teeth on both edges that cut on the pull stroke, rather than the push stroke of Western saws, and a small dovetail saw.*

Both the cross-cut and rip saw are tapered along their width, but back saws are rectangular. While the other saws cut with the blade at an angle, a back saw is designed to be used at an angle only at the beginning of a cut. Once the kerf is established across the board, the cutting teeth are moved parallel to the surface being sawn, so that it cuts a straight line across the whole board.

Always draw a guideline with a square or marking gauge before making any kind of saw cut. Remember, with Western-style saws, the cut is on the push stroke. The area of the board most likely to tear out is where the teeth leave the blades, so make any guide marks on the best side of the board and cut from that side. Any tearing should be on the less attractive face.

In drawing your guidelines, whenever possible draw a line across the face of the board and down its edge, so you can use both lines to guide the blade. That will help you start a cut that is true on both faces. Once the cut is started, the blade will tend to follow the original kerf and run fairly true.

After laying out the line, the important thing is to start the cut correctly. Hold the saw handle firmly, but do not try to strangle it. Extend

*Left: Start the cut with the backsaw at a fairly low angle (top), and extend the cut across the board, until the saw teeth are running parallel to the surface of the board (bottom).*

your index finger straight out along the side of the handle to help guide your motion. Put the knuckle of the thumb of your other hand against the blade of the saw to steady it. Some workers put a T-square alongside the board to make sure the blade is perpendicular to the surface of the wood.

Start the cut with the saw blade held at a fairly low angle. Cut on the waste side of the line. Pull backward on the corner of the board, then deepen the notch with these backward cuts. Do not push down too hard – a sharp saw will pretty much cut on its own weight – and do not force the blade; let it slide smoothly. Once the kerf is well established, switch to forward strokes. As you cut, listen to the saw and feel the vibrations. If everything is really rough, you are probably using the tool at the wrong angle.

## A SIMPLE CLAMP

Wedges offer a low-cost way to secure work to your bench. Simply secure one side of the piece against a pair of bench dogs, as shown here, or a cleat clamped to your work table. Place more dogs or another cleat on the other side and drive in a pair of opposing wedges. As the wedges slide past each other, they push against the wood and lock it between the cleats or dogs. A slight tap with a mallet secures the assembly. Another tap in the opposite direction releases everything.

Another common saw designed to cut curves is the coping saw, a metal frame tensioning a very slender, flexible blade. The blade is mounted with the teeth facing the handle, and it cuts on the pull stroke. When cutting with a coping saw, hold the blade straight and square to the surface, so that it cuts across the whole width of the piece. This saw is generally used for thin materials, so this is not much of a problem.

*Left: A carpenter's cross-cut saw is good for straight cuts across the board.*
*Far Left: The thin blade of a coping saw is designed to cut curves.*

## Chisels

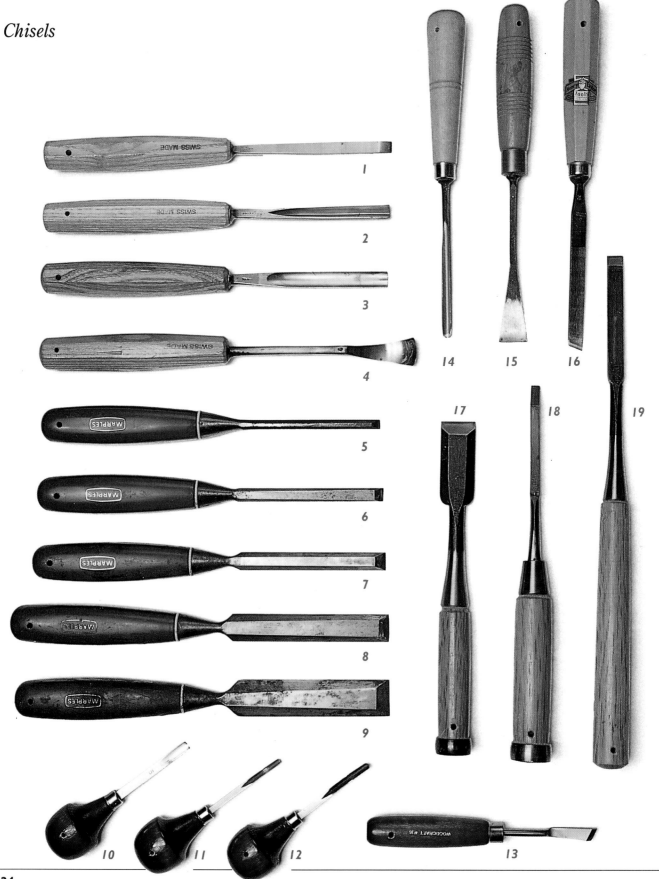

1
2
3
4
5
6
7
8
9
10
11
12
13
14
15
16
17
18
19

*Left: The common chisel types.*
*Carving tools*
*1. Thin carver's chisel*
*2. Paring tool*
*3. Gouge*
*4. Spoon gouge*
*5–9. Carpenter's chisels*
*10–13. Small carving tools*
*14. Veiner*
*15. Fish-tail*
*16. Skew*

*Japanese laminated chisels*
*17. Carpenter's chisel*
*18. Mortice chisel*
*19. Long paring chisel*

Chisels are simply heavy, flat pieces of tempered steel with a handle on one end and a sharpened bevelled edge on the other side. They can be pushed through the wood with the force of your hand, or tapped with a mallet.

As with most cutting tools, do not make the mistake of substituting force for a sharp edge. Learn to sharpen your tools as discussed in Chapter 9. This is a simple skill once

you get the hang of it. In addition to making your workshop life much easier, the ability to sharpen knives will make you pretty popular in the kitchen.

Do not lunge with the chisel or hold the work with one hand while you try to chisel with the other. Clamp the wood to your bench to minimize the chances of hurting yourself. Also, make the cuts by keeping both hands on the chisel,

*Right: Chisels with flat blades shear off thin shavings with the grain (top), but tend to tear wood fibres across the grain (bottom).*

behind the cutting edge. You reduce the chances of hurting yourself if both hands are on the chisel. Always cut away from yourself. If you drop a chisel, do not try to catch it or stick your foot out to prevent it from slamming into the floor.

For a start, just get a couple of carpenter's butt chisels, in widths between 6 mm (¼ in) and 25 mm (1 in) Many woodworkers cut both with and across the grain with the chisel bevel up and use the flat back of the tool to guide the cutting edge. I often find that working with the bevel down makes it easier to control the cut and prevent the chisel from diving into the wood, as can quickly happen when the bevel is up, especially if you are cutting across the grain. For paring cuts across the end grain, as often used when trimming dovetails, place the flat of the blade on the line and the bevel on the waste side and drive the tool with your hand. Once you get going, you might consider buying some more specialized chisels, especially if you do a lot of morticing. Mortice chisels are heavier than butt chisels and are made for prying out waste in deep cuts. Carving chisels work well both with and across the grain when you want to hollow a section of a board. You can drive the carving tools with either your hand or a mallet.

*Below: The chisel must be extremely sharp to pare the end grain section of a dovetail joint.*
*Below right: A mallet is often used to drive the tool.*

*Left: Gouges with curved cutting edges remove stock quickly, both with the grain, or across the grain.*

*Below (left to right) carpenter's mallet, steel-shafted claw hammer, cross-peen hammer, and a nail set.*

## Hammers and mallets

Mallets are pretty useful for woodworkers. I prefer the carver's mallet for tapping on chisels. The round shape of the mallet means you get a good solid contact with the chisel handle no matter how you hold the mallet. You do not have to keep looking to see if the mallet head is properly aligned as you would if you used a hammer. Also, the wooden mallet will not damage the chisel handle in the way a steel hammer would. Find a mallet that is comfortable for you. You do not need to hit the chisel very hard, so I prefer a 450 g (1 lb) model.

Any ordinary 450 g (1 lb) carpenter's hammer will do fine for most applications. Mine is used mostly for driving in small brads and finishing nails. For assembly work, a dead-blow hammer works well. I first learned about them from a car body refinisher who liked the way they did not bounce back when he hammered on sheet metal.

## Planes

Planes are among my favourite hand tools. There is something magical about they way they shoot out cascading clouds of wispy thin shavings as they flatten and smooth timber.

In the eighteenth century, cabinetmakers would probably have hundreds of planes, each designed to cut specific moulding shapes and details. Now most of those shapes can be duplicated more quickly and more smoothly with mechanized routers and, in larger workshops, by heavy-duty shapers.

The planes I use most are a small block plane, a number 5 Record Marples plane and a number 7 jointer plane. I also like the all-wood coffin plane and the scrub plane (the one with the banana-like front handle), which is good for removing a lot of stock quickly. Many woodworkers spend a lot of time tuning up a plane, but I have been fortunate to have planes that work well once the blade is sharp. There is no substitute for sharpness here.

As you can see in the picture, planes are not terribly complex. Basically a body with a flat bottom or sole, sides machined perpendicular to the bottom, front and rear handles, an angled assembly for supporting and moving the cutting iron. The actual cutting unit includes a blade, a chip breaker and a cap iron that holds the blade to the plane body. When you buy one, you should get a leaflet that will explain how it works.

In going over the manufacturer's directions, pay attention to setting the chip breaker and the depth of cut. Set

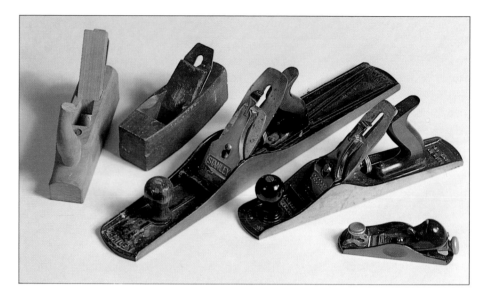

the chip breaker close to the edge for a fine cut, and back it off slightly for coarser cuts. You may have to flatten the edge of the chip breaker on a whetstone to ensure the pieces fit together tightly. Set the blade for a light cut. Do not try to take too much off in a single pass. One way to check how much blade is protruding and to square it to the sole of the plane is to sight down the sole.

*Top: Longer planes are best for finishing and shorter ones for roughing out. Shown from left: a scrub plane for removing wood rapidly, a small coffin plane, a long jointer plane, a smoothing plane, and a block plane.*

*Above: The anatomy of a plane; main body, blade, chip breaker, and cap iron.*

The important thing is to plane with the grain. There are all kinds of tricks to learning how to tell which way is right. Experience is the best guide, but until you get some, try this system that I learned from Bruce Hoadley, a wood technologist in Massachusetts. Look at the end grain and see how the growth rings are curved. You can think of growth rings as a series of circles surrounding a centre core called a pith. Outside of the largest circle would be the bark of a tree. On the pith side of a board, the side facing the concave section of the ring, plane toward the points of the figure. On the bark side, plane the other way, away from the points. The ultimate test is if the wood tears. If it does, switch directions and look at the board carefully to see if you can recognize any features that will help you handle another similar board in the future.

Sometimes the grains on a wood like maple will be very tight and interlocked, so they are very prone to tearing out. In this case, set the plane for the finest cut possible and work slowly.

I do not have any magic system for planing. Basically for initial cuts I hold the plane flat on the surface at about a 45-degree angle to the length of a board and push the plane straight up the board, overlapping strokes as I go. As the surface becomes smoother, I usually reduce the angle until it is just about parallel to the edge of the board for the final passes.

Even the best job of planing will leave slight ridges on the surface.

*Above: Sight down the plane to determine how far the blade protrudes and whether the cutting edge is set parallel to the bottom or the sole.*

*Above: In the finishing stages of planing, the tool is moved parallel or nearly parallel to the edges of the panel.*

*Right: The edge of the chip breaker is set close to the cutting edge for a fine cut. The cap iron tightens the screw holding the pieces together.*

These can be removed with a pad sander, although some workers like the hand-planed effect and the crisp look of wood cut with a razor-sharp plane blade.

A long-body plane, like a jointer plane, is best for squaring up the edge of a board. Take light passes, eliminating the high spots first. When the edge is flat, you should be able to make a single pass along the edge of the entire board. Use your hand and fingers to support the plane and ensure a square cut.

## Other useful hand tools

A **nail set**, like the ones shown (page 26), is handy whenever working with brads and small finishing nails. A typical set contains four steel punches, each about the size of a pencil cut in half. Each punch has a full-diameter end that you hammer on; the other end is tapered down to a point. Match the diameter of the point to the size of nail or brad.

When you are working with nails, you do not want the nails to stick out of the wood, but if you drive them down too far with a hammer, you are likely to dent the surface and leave a series of depressions, often called "hoof marks". These trophies of your over-energetic hammer will seem to dent the surface like craters once you apply varnish or other finish. The better method is to drive the brad to just above the surface, then use a nail set of the proper size to drive it down until it is slightly below the surface. You can use putty or

woodfiller to cover the little hole.

A couple of inexpensive scraping tools are also handy in your tool box for rounding over edges of boards or tenons. Ordinary **machinist's files** work well on wood, and can produce a surprisingly fine edge. Just remember the file only cuts on the push stroke; do not drag it back on the surface or it will dull quickly. Files are effective on flat surfaces, as well as curved. This operation is sometimes called draw-filing. Hold the handle in your left hand and slide the file toward your body.

*Above: A rasp, which generally has larger teeth than a file, makes a much more aggressive cut.*

*Top: Files and rasps are tough abrasive tools. A file can quickly round over and smooth the edge of a board.*

*Left: A file can be drawn along an edge to flatten the surface.*

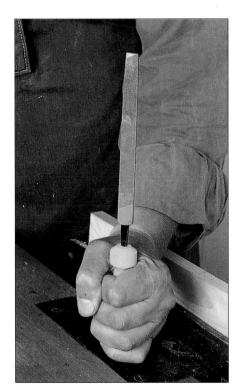

*Above: Files are easier, and safer, to use if they are fitted with handles, plus it's fun. Fit the file tang into a hole bored in the handle, slam the handle down on a bench a couple of times and the file magically slides in.*

**Rasps** have much more distinctly pointed teeth and cut much faster. If you have a lot of material to remove, use a rasp, then a file to remove the scratches left by the rasp, and finally sand the board. To protect your hands when filing, it is a good idea to put a handle on the tool. You can create something special yourself, buy a handle or just use a section of dowel. Drill a hole into the wood, as deep as the length of the tang, which is the tapering tail-like section on one end of the file. Use a bit with a diameter equal to the width of the tang at its midpoint. Insert the tang into the handle, then slam the handle, butt first, down onto a hard surface. The force will draw the tang into the wood.

Another abrasive tool is called the **Surform**. This has a plastic handle supporting a flexible piece of metal with teeth cut in it. Surforms are available in various sizes and shapes and cut very well, shearing off fine shavings. When they are dull you do not even have to sharpen them – just replace the metal cutting surface.

*Right: Surforms and similar tools have a metal, screen-like cutter that can quickly shear off a mass of shavings.*

# 9 *Sharpening Tools*

Sharpening is one of the most daunting tasks for many woodworkers. I have never figured out why. My great grandfather could sharpen and hone a razor well enough to shave without scraping the flesh off his chin, so I always assumed it was just one of the skills we all had to learn. Now, other methods of shaving are available, but sharp tools are still essential in other fields.

One of the main reasons for sharpening your tools is that a sharp tool is safer than a dull one. You do not have to use a sharp tool with as much force, so you can concentrate on control and accuracy. Plus, for the woodworker, a sharp cutting edge shears wood fibres leaving a crisp, glistening surface that enhances the appearance of any object. If you are really good at sharpening and handling your tools, you can also relieve yourself of the task of sanding every surface to death. Sanded surfaces do not take a finish as well as a cut one, and sanding is never pleasant.

My basic sharpening equipment is simple – a standard two-wheel grindstone on a knock-together stand, plus an assortment of handstones. I have both oilstones, which were the first type I used, and Japanese waterstones, which I rely on more and more. There are advantages to both types. Oilstones are readily available, wear well and can be used to sharpen both flat and curved edges. Japanese stones are much softer than oilstones, so they have to be handled a little

**Above: A standard two-wheel grindstone.**

**Right: Flattening a Japanese stone with emery paper.**

more carefully to prevent gouging. I flatten mine every day, with emery paper glued to a piece of plate glass. Also, I do not use them to sharpen carving tools, because the shapes of the tools seem to gouge into the stone as well as into wood, making the stone useless for sharpening chisels and plane blades.

For sharpening plane blades and

chisels, I prefer the fast-cutting action of the Japanese waterstones. I start out with one 800 grit stone, then progress through several grades to 8,000 grit Gold stone, for a final mirror-like finish. There is no special trick to sharpening on the stones. Flatten the stone on the glass and paper, then rest the blade on the stone so its bevel is flat on the abrasive surface. The stones should be soaked in water before you begin, and may have to be sprayed with water as you go along. A simple plant sprayer works well when you need to wet the surface.

I hold my wrist cocked at a slight angle to support the bevel without rocking or tipping. As added protection I sometimes use the fingers of the other hand to steady and guide the blade near the cutting edge. Slowly move the blade back and forth, being careful not to rock the bevel. Move in different places along the stone, in slow deliberate strokes to get maximum sharpening effect without wearing out a particular section of the stone. After working for a while on the bevel, I hold the tool flat on its back and hone the back edge. This ensures the back is flat and true to the cutting edge and provides a true reference for the chisel when cutting dovetails or paring a tenon cheek.

As you work with the waterstones, you will notice a slurry of dissolved stone and metal on the stone. Do not worry about it. That is actually a major part of the cutting action. If it gets too dry, just spray on a little more water and continue. Experience will tell you how dry or wet you want the stone for best performances.

One warning, the water makes the

*Above: Hold your wrist at a right angle when sharpening a chisel.*

*Left: Don't forget to hone the back edge of the chisel.*

stones feel very cool and it is difficult to imagine that the mud-like slurry is really cutting. This is especially true if you are used to working with oilstones, which tend to be more abrasive to the touch. Run your fingers across an oilstone and you can feel what does the cutting.

The first time I used waterstones I was just enjoying the whole process until I noticed that the stone was splotched with red. It was blood from my fingertips. In the wet mud I had

not realized that I was abrading my fingertips as I worked on the tool. The instructor of the class I was attending told me that that was a common occurrence in beginners' classes.

Techniques for moving the tools along oilstones are very similar, but I find the process takes longer. Keep the stones moistened with oil to help float off metal fragments from the sharpening. Oilstones need to be flattened less often than waterstones, so you do not have to worry about it until you see a concavity developing on the surface. This can take years.

Woodworkers debate whether it is better to have water or oil in the workshop for sharpening. I find them both a little messy, and the oil often seems to leave ugly metal stains on the wood and hands it comes in contact with. Water seems easy to remove, but you must be careful to dry all the metal parts thoroughly after sharpening to make sure there is not enough moisture on the metal to cause rust.

I avoid using the grinder as much as possible, except for high-speed steel turning tools which are tough enough to endure grinding without damage. The grinder spins at about 3,700 rpm, so it is easy to burn the edge, turning the metal blue and removing the temper or edge-holding ability of the metal. Use a light touch when grinding and have a container of water handy to dip the edge frequently to prevent overheating.

The wheel will run cooler if you dress it frequently to remove glazed-on metal particles. The dressing stick will also flatten the wheel, making a better surface for grinding.

If you have damaged an edge, as often happens when it is dropped on the floor or contacts metal, a grinder is a lifesaver. Also, sometimes it is necessary to change the angle of the bevel or make some other major modification. Just take it easy, especially if you have a lot of metal to remove. If you have taken out a chunk of the edge, for example, you probably will have to grind down the whole edge flat to straighten it. Go slowly and quench the blade often. Also check the edge with a T-square to make sure everything is true. Once

the chip is removed, you will probably have a cutting edge only slightly less crude than a butter knife. Now proceed to regrind the edge. When you have a fairly good edge, switch to handstones for final sharpening and honing.

You can make or buy all sorts of guides for supporting the grinding process, but I have found the standard rests that come with the grinder to be adequate for most jobs. If you are working with a lot of wide-plane irons, though, you might want to extend the rest or build an auxiliary fence of wood. I just rest my fingers on the tool rest and guide the blade on top of my fingers. This takes a little practice, so in the beginning you might be better just to set the angle of the support to the proper angle to ensure that all is well. You can use special bevels of different applications, but generally I work with about 25- to 30-degree angles. At these angles the length of the bevel is about twice the thickness of the blade. Sometimes workers will use a sharper angle for softwoods or a steep one for hard-

woods. Do not be afraid to experiment once you get going. The bevel that came with the tool is not sacred.

Do not neglect your sharpening duties. I think one good rule is never to let your tools get dull. If you hone them as you work you will avoid having to spend a lot of time working on each blade, and they will always be keen enough to give good results.

If you cannot seem to learn how to sharpen, visit your local tool supplier and ask him to show you some of the mechanical guides he sells. Some of them are specially designed for chisels

*Below: A dressing stick will help flatten the grinding wheel.*

or blades and feature a roller to carry the assembly over the stone and a rigid gripping device for holding the tool at the proper angle, rock steady. These sharpening guides are very expensive, but a lot of people swear by them. Also, some of the newer horizontal grinders, which use waterstones, are very efficient and have special guides for ensuring accurate grinding.

*Top: Proceed carefully when grinding down the entire edge of a tool.*

*Middle: Use a T-square to check that the chisel edge is square and true.*

*Bottom: Use the standard angle for the support guide on the grinder until you feel confident enough to use your own judgement.*

# 10 *A Primer on Power Tool Use*

## *Table-saw*

The table-saw is one of the most valuable tools in the workshop – and the most dangerous. It is fast, powerful and can do a wide variety of cuts with great accuracy. But it must always be treated with respect.

There are so many types and sizes of table-saws on the market that it would be impossible to cover them all in a single chapter. Depend on the owner's manual for your tool. Set up the saw as directed and pay special attention to recommendations on safety as you go.

Basically, the tool consists of a metal table with an elongated oval opening in the centre. Underneath the table is a complex assembly, called a trunnion, which supports a horizontal shaft. One end of the shaft is connected by a belt-and-pulley arrangement to an electric motor. The other end has threads and a flange for bolting on a blade, which is mounted so that the cutting teeth rotate towards the operator. The trunnion assembly can be adjusted to change the blade's angle and depth of cut, by raising or lowering the blade in the table.

The opening in the top is much wider than the blade that comes up through it. Much of the space is filled with a throat plate, a metal oval machined to fit into the table. It also has a slot to allow the saw blade to protrude. Many throat plates leave about 9-mm ($^3/_8$-in) open space on each side of the blade, so many woodworkers replace the metal plate

with a wooden one, which can be sized to fit more closely along the sides of the blade and provide more support to the wood being cut. An important part of a throat plate or auxiliary guard is a splitting or riving knife, which is located behind the blade and slides into the kerf of the just-cut stock. The knife prevents the just-cut wood from pinching the blade, and possibly being kicked back towards the operator. Some guards also are fitted with anti-kickback fingers, too, to minimize chances of pieces being thrown back by the blade. Check your owner's manual for more information. Special throat plates are also needed to accept special cutters for the table-saw, such

*Above: A table-saw is the heart of many workshops, because of its power and versatility. But it must always be treated with respect. Guards have been removed for greater clarity here, but guards, push sticks and other safety devices should always be used when you're working.*

as housing cutters and moulding heads. Do not use these speciality cutters without a protective throat plate.

Two main types of guides are used to support and control wood as it is being cut. Bars and tubes at the front and back of the saw support a fence, a rectangular bar several inches high which sits perpendicular to the table. When you rip a piece of wood, that is, cut it along its length, the fence guides the stock as it is being pushed by the blade. Never try to do this operation, or any other, freehand on the saw; the chances that you will lose control are too great.

Your owner's manual will tell you how to adjust the fence perpendicular to the table. It can also be adjusted to be perfectly parallel to the blade or skewed just a whisker on the end behind the blade. This slight offset makes it easier for the wood to pass off the saw after being cut. Wood only needs to contact the fence before the cut.

The second guide is a mitre gauge, which runs in slots milled into the table on each side of the blade opening. The gauge has a tongue that fits into the slot and supports a carriage that can be set perpendicular or at some other angle to the tongue. The gauge supports the wood as it is cross-cut on the saw. Check your manual for instructions on setting the gauge. For most work, it is very important for the face of the gauge to be set exactly perpendicular to the tongue and thus perpendicular to the blade.

Because the mitre gauge is only a few inches wide, some woodworkers will screw an auxiliary fence to the gauge, to give more support to pieces during the cut. Also, you can make plywood carriages to support pieces during the cross-cut. Most of these carriages are mounted on a plywood base, equipped with cleats that run in the saw-table slots. The plywood is aligned with the slots and the front of the table, then fences can be screwed to the base to achieve the desired

angle of cut, usually 90 degrees for most work or 45 degrees for mitre cuts.

For accurate cuts, it is necessary to set the blade accurately. Most of the time 90-degree cuts are needed, so the blade must be perpendicular to the saw table. This can be set by holding a square against the blade and using the saw's blade-tilt mechanism to move the blade into alignment. Once the angle is set, lock it in place, using whatever mechanism is provided on your saw.

The trick in aligning the blade is to fit the square on a flat area between the teeth. If you look at the blade, you will see how the teeth bend slightly to the left or right, so it is important to make all your adjustments from the flat of the blade, not from the teeth.

Regardless of what cut you are making, keep your hands away from

*Above: A T-square is an ideal tool for setting the fence on a joint exactly parallel to the flat table of the tool.*

the blade. And make sure you do not have any loose clothing or jewellery or anything else that can tangle in the blade and pull you in. Use push sticks and feather boards, like the ones shown in the diagram, to keep your fingers away from the blade. Also avoid wood with loose knots. The blade can catch them and throw them back with amazing force. Remember, that blade is running at about 3,700 rpm.

Throwback is always a potential danger. Never stand directly behind the blade. Stand aside, so if something does fly back you will be safe. A thin strip can come back with enough force to stick into a plasterboard wall.

As another safety precaution, for thin stock set the blade height so that the points protrude above the piece being cut. If the blade is too low, there is a risk of throwback.

Also, always use the guards provided. Protect yourself.

Blades for table-saws come in a staggering array of types and configurations. For a start, try combination blades with 40 points per 25 mm (1 in). These blades work well for both ripping and cross-cutting, and make fairly smooth cuts.

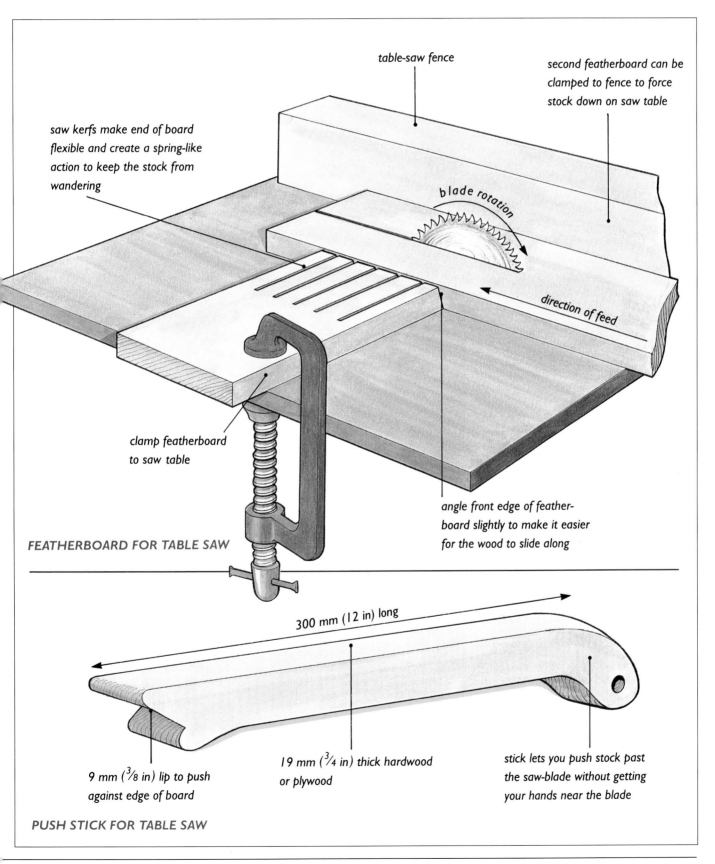

table-saw fence

second featherboard can be clamped to fence to force stock down on saw table

saw kerfs make end of board flexible and create a spring-like action to keep the stock from wandering

blade rotation

direction of feed

clamp featherboard to saw table

angle front edge of featherboard slightly to make it easier for the wood to slide along

**FEATHERBOARD FOR TABLE SAW**

300 mm (12 in) long

9 mm ($^3/_8$ in) lip to push against edge of board

19 mm ($^3/_4$ in) thick hardwood or plywood

stick lets you push stock past the saw-blade without getting your hands near the blade

**PUSH STICK FOR TABLE SAW**

## Jointer

The jointer is the most dangerous machine in the amateur workshop. It is, however, a precision tool that will help you work more efficiently because it accurately establishes the flat and square reference surfaces needed to size and shape most furniture components.

Most jointers have two tables, flanking a cutter head connected by a belt to an electric motor. On some jointers both tables can be moved up or down in relation to the cutter head, but some only allow you to move the table to the right of the cutter, called the infeed table. The other table, the one that supports the wood after the cut is called the outfeed table.

For accurate cuts, the outfeed table must be at exactly the same height as the knives. If you cannot adjust the level of the table, you must align the knives in the cutter head with the table before you begin work. Check your owner's manual. If you do not take the time to make this adjustment all your work will be tapered.

On most small workshop jointers the depth of cut is controlled by raising or lowering the infeed table in relation to the cutter head. A jointer

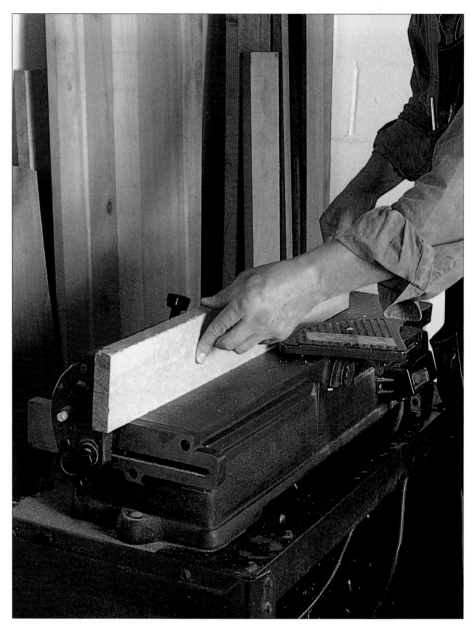

*Above: Checking the edge of the board for square.*

can take a fairly heavy cut, but do not be tempted to do so. Precision and a fine finish are the keys here, so make your cuts in the 2- to 3-mm ($\frac{1}{16}$- to $\frac{1}{8}$-in) range.

Like the table-saw, the jointer is usually set to make 90-degree cuts. Set the fence on the jointer with a square, just as you did with the table-saw blade. Set the fence with the square on the infeed table.

Once the fence is aligned with the

*Above: To square the edge of a board, hold the stock firmly against the fence and table, and slide it over the cutter head. Once the wood passes the cutter, move your hand up to keep the edge down on the outfeed table.*

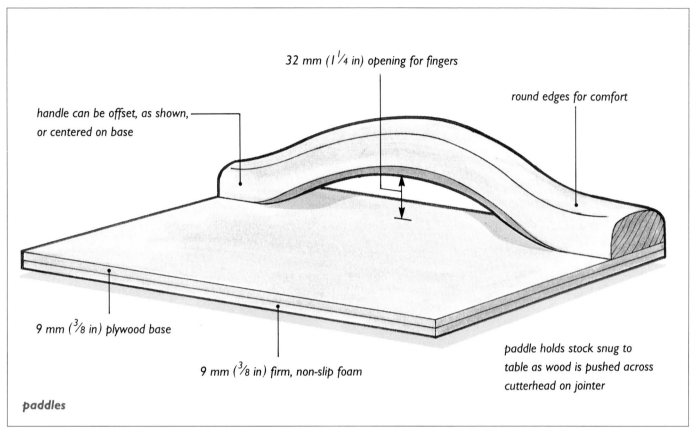

*32 mm (1 ¼ in) opening for fingers*

*round edges for comfort*

*handle can be offset, as shown, or centered on base*

*9 mm (³⁄₈ in) plywood base*

*9 mm (³⁄₈ in) firm, non-slip foam*

*paddle holds stock snug to table as wood is pushed across cutterhead on jointer*

**paddles**

table, it takes practice to square the edges of the board, one of the common operations done on the jointer.

Hold the board on edge on the infeed table. Place the flat face of the board against the fence and push the piece forward. Once the end of the board passes the cutter head and is supported by the outfeed table, move your hand forward to the outfeed section and push down on the board there. Move the board through your hands. Once it is registered on to the outfeed table, you can work slowly: just keep the piece moving steadily.

Always joint with the grain. If you hear wood chattering and tearing with the cut, you are going the wrong way. Reverse the board and start again. Continue taking light passes along the edge of the board until you can get one continuous cut along the entire

length. Check for square with a T-square. When you have a little more experience you will not need to check the boards, but in the beginning it will help you to detect mistakes right away, before you go any further.

If the board has a concave edge, I usually make a couple of passes to remove the high points, then do the whole edge. I have seen other workers begin with the convex side and joint the high centre spot away, then do the whole edge. Regardless of your method of work, never joint the edge of a piece narrower than 75 to 100 mm (3 to 4 in) without using a push stick.

A jointer is also used to flatten one face of a board. You can do a fairly wide board if you have a jointer at least 150 mm (6 in) wide. The technique is the same as for edge jointing, except you have to work

slowly because you are taking off a much wider strip with each pass. Remove the high spots first, then do the whole board. Once you have one flat face, you can run the board through a thickness planer, with the flat face on the planer table and making the second face parallel to the first.

Always use a push stick or a foam-covered paddle when face jointing. The paddles are just plywood sections with a handle on one side and a foam covering on the other. The foam grips the wood well enough for you to push the board along. I usually use two of the paddles, so my fingers never get near the knives. Never attempt to push the end of the board along with your fingers.

The sequence for flattening and edging timber will be discussed further in chapter 11.

# 11 Stock Preparation

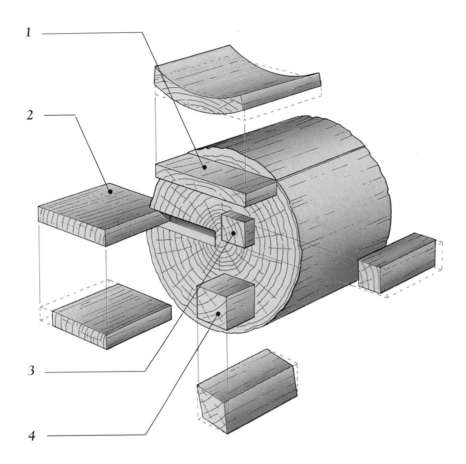

*Above: 1, wide boards will shrink more in width than length or thickness, and cup away from the tree's original heart; 2, the rings at right angles to the surface cause minimum shrinkage and distortion; 3, again perpendicular rings mean optimum dimensional stability; 4, square sections with the growth rings diagonally across them will go rhomboid*

Converting a pile of rough-sawn, warped and cracked timber into a stack of furniture-grade timber can be an exhausting task, especially if you work alone and do not have a full arsenal of power tools. Though essential, this bull work is not really crucial to the craftsmanship that makes or breaks a piece. Do not feel guilty about buying your timber surfaced on two or four sides – or for paying an extra fee to have your supplier rough out the stock for you. If you want to make an omelette, most of us do not feel guilty about buying eggs and milk provided by someone else. The art is actually in the cooking, not in buying the ingredients.

Most woodworking projects require timber that is flat, reasonably free of defects, with straight and square edges that are parallel to each other. Most of the boards offered for sale are available in (8-ft) lengths, a good length for most jobs. But few projects actually involve timber that long, so it does not make sense to flatten, edge, and dress 2440-mm (8-ft) boards when the longest component you need is 300–900 mm (1–3 ft) long.

My basic procedure is to cut the boards up into rough lengths slightly longer than the pieces I need. This cutting-out process, in addition to making it easier to mill the wood, also makes it easy to eliminate ugly streaks or structural defects from the wood. Perfectly clear defect-free boards are very rare and expensive. And they are often not as attractive as some of the more ordinary ones.

A couple of cautions – always rough-cut the pieces longer than you need. You want to make sure that the dressed boards are adequate for your project. If you cut a board too short, you will have to start again with another one. Hence the old adage: "Measure twice, cut once." A margin of 10 to 15 per cent should be more

than adequate to start. Also, do not even try to use the final 50–75 mm (2–3 in) on the end of each board – usually these sections are badly cracked, filled with dirt and generally unreliable. Relegate them to the scrap pile right away and get to work on the good stuff.

Also, do not cut the sections too short. Some power tools cannot be used safely with short lengths of wood. It is generally dangerous to joint a piece less than 250–380 mm (10–15 in) long. Many planers, because of the arrangement of the cutter head and the rollers which carry the wood through the machine, cannot handle very short pieces. If you need a 125 mm (5 in) piece, it is better to mill a 300–380 mm (12–15 in) piece, then cut it to length.

Once you have your rough-cut components, the next step is to flatten one face. This flat face establishes the reference surface, from which you will establish all the other surfaces. You can flatten the face with a jointer, as previously discussed, or with a hand plane.

Pick the surface you want to work with, attach the board to your bench and begin planing away the high spots. Ideally you want to remove enough of the wood, so that the face of the board will be flat from end to end and edge to edge. As you are working, use the edge of the plane as a gauge to check that you are flattening the surface.

I sometimes remove the high spots of the board with a hand plane, then

*Right: stacks of timber in a large commercial kiln. The operator is selecting a sample from the middle of the pile to check it for moisture content; these are small-section boards which are quite likely to have been dried once already, before conversion to this size.*

*Below left: "closed piled" air-drying keeps the gaps between the boards small. This avoids distortion due to different drying rates between the surface and the centre.*

*Below: a "stickered" pile for air-drying; timber for kilning must also be stacked like this.*

*Above: Preparing wood stock with a thickness planer.*

refine the surface by running it over the overhand planer. It seems just as fast as doing the whole thing on the overhand planer, and keeps my planing techniques tuned up.

Winding sticks, two identical pieces of wood with a line across the middle of each, are also good for gauging warp or cup. Place one stick across one edge of the board, the other a little farther up the length of the piece. By comparing the tilt of the lines marked across the middle of the boards, you can gauge where more wood has to be removed.

Once you have a flat face, joint the edge of the board, as described in chapter 9. Just make sure to run the flat face of the board against the fence of the overhand planer. Now you have one flat face and one square edge to it.

You can make the second edge of the board parallel to the jointed edge by ripping the piece on the table saw. Again, run the flattened face of the board down on the table and the squared edge against the fence. Set the fence to cut the board to the desired width. After ripping the piece to width, you can run the piece through the thicknesser to make the second face parallel to the first, or do the job with a hand plane. The best way to do this is to set a marking gauge to the desired thickness, then score a line all around the board, so you can see where wood must be removed to bring both faces parallel.

To flatten a board, start with a scrub plane, which is equipped with a tougue-shaped blade that cuts across the grain quickly, and go on to a number 07 fore plane for flatness and a smoothing plane to finish.

If I have a planer to work with, I generally flatten the second side, then turn the board over and run the hand-planed side through to remove any of the irregularities that might have been left by the hand plane. If you have done a good job with the hand plane this step is unnecessary. Any tool marks from the plane can be removed with a sander later.

*Above: Using a hand plane to flatten a board.*

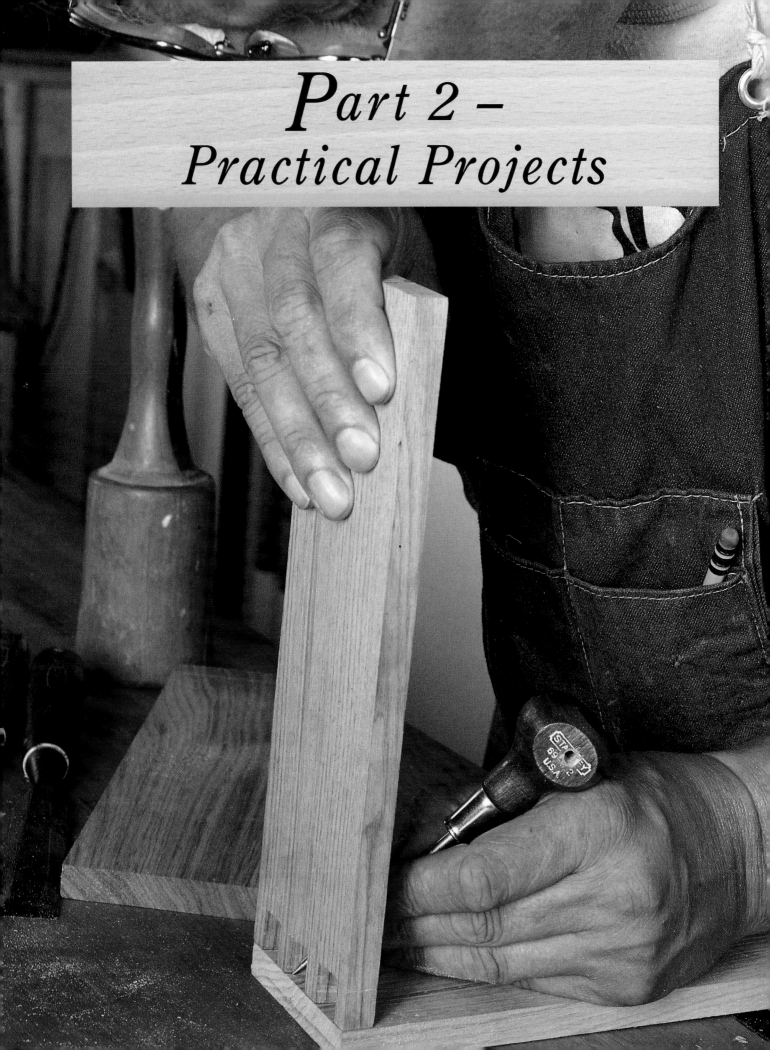

# Part 2 –
# Practical Projects

*J*oinery is the art of putting pieces of wood together to make strong, attractive and functional objects. Each of the joints is fairly traditional, a time-tested method of work. Some are for very specific applications, but most can be used in a variety of ways.

As you work on mastering the joints, think a little about the strengths and weaknesses of each. Why is a mortise and tenon stronger than a dowel? How much glue surface does it offer? Do the mating surfaces involve long-grain to long-grain connections that make for a strong glue-up or is one of the surfaces an end grain that glues poorly? Are there mechanical features, such as shoulders or splines, that add to the strength of the joint?

In addition to working with the joints, think about them as you look at a piece of furniture. What joint has been used where? If the details of the joinery are visible, as with through dovetails, what does this add to the look of the piece? What did the maker have in mind?

Several different methods are outlined for most joints. Most can be cut by hand, by machine or with a combination of hand and machine techniques. Use the method that makes the most sense for you. Do practice the joint on scrap wood before risking your good wood.

Every time you make a joint you will learn something valuable, although in the beginning it may seem that it takes all your skill and patience just to complete the thing. Do not get discouraged. Before long, you will be more concerned with degrees of perfection than with whether or not you are able to do something.

The joints are all arranged around different projects. The project becomes, in effect, just a means to demonstrate how a joint can be used. Measurements given are approximations, just preliminary guidelines for proportions. Adapt the situation to meet your individual needs. Just remember that each joint has to be suited to its intended use and cut carefully so that all the pieces fit together snugly and squarely. If you have to hammer things together, generally something is wrong and you are well on your way to breaking the joint or creating an object that will fall apart in the near future. Only the gentlest of persuasion should be required.

There has been no attempt to arrange joints in order of difficulty. Many of the first demonstrations seem easy, because they rely on basic sawing or chiselling skills you have probably already been practising. Actually, even the more complex joints rely on the same skills.

## GARBAGE IN, GARBAGE OUT

I am generally not a fan of the computer jargon in our electronic age, but the admonition of "Garbage in, garbage out" is a good guideline for woodworkers. Computer programmers know that if you start out with poor material there is not much a computer can do to change it into something wonderful.

The same is painfully true of woodworking. It will seem tempting just to take that stack of nice-looking boards straight from the timber yard and start cutting and laying out joints without worrying about details, such as whether the edges are square or the pieces flat and the same thickness – whether those knots are really solid... I know I have done it, and I have always been sorry.

Take the time to square up the wood, establish reference surfaces, and select the best-looking pieces for the most visible parts of your project. Make sure the grain patterns harmonize with what you have in mind. Lay everything out accurately. Make sure that the saw fence or mitre gauge has not been knocked out of alignment since your last job.

Cutting joints in out-of-square stock is a nuisance. Assembling a piece with out-of-alignment components can be a real nightmare. You will have to invest a lot of hard work to get everything together, and the resulting assembly probably will be out of square anyway. Pay attention to the details and do it right the first time.

# A Simple Bookcase

*A bookcase is a good project for beginners. Every house seems to need another shelf unit, and you can build one with fairly inexpensive timber, so you do not have to invest a lot of money. Bookcases usually do not have any difficult angles to work with and the joints are fairly simple.*

## HOUSINGS

Housing joints are frequently seen on bookcases and inside chests. The joint provides a reliable way to join a horizontal component to some type of vertical support, although it is often used to insert dividers into a horizontal piece.

The housing itself is a square-bottomed groove cut across the width of a board. The groove must be wide enough to accept the thickness of the board that will be joined to it, generally at a 90-degree angle.

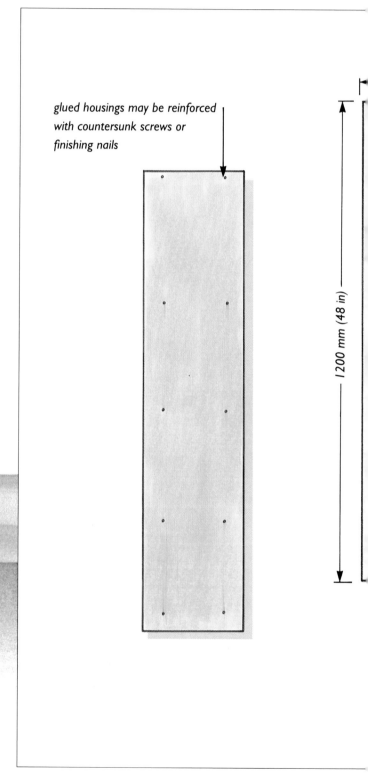

glued housings may be reinforced with countersunk screws or finishing nails

1200 mm (48 in)

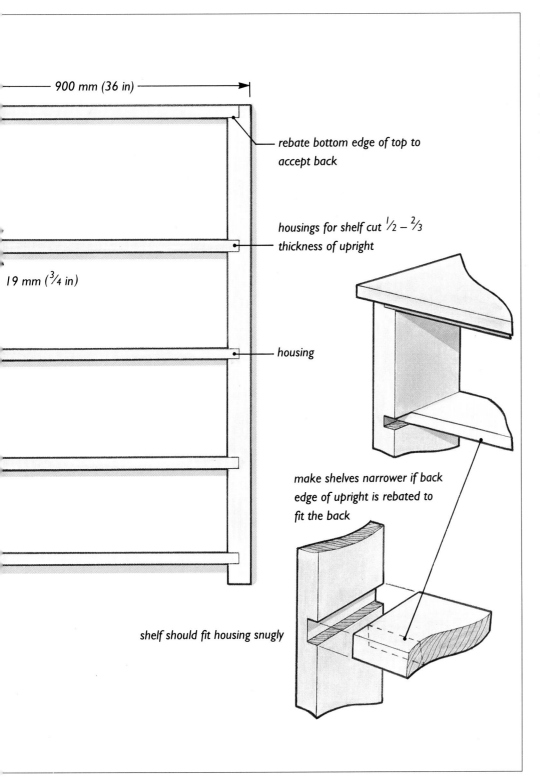

900 mm (36 in)

rebate bottom edge of top to accept back

housings for shelf cut ½ – ⅔ thickness of upright

19 mm (¾ in)

housing

make shelves narrower if back edge of upright is rebated to fit the back

shelf should fit housing snugly

Removing enough material to fit a 19 mm (¾ in) thick shelf into the vertical up-right, for example, weakens the upright, but this weakness is eliminated when the mating board is glued in place. In most uses, the weight will be down, so most of the stress on the shelf is absorbed by the bottom of the housing.

As the housing must be wide enough to accept the full thickness of a shelf, the groove must be wider than the width of a standard saw-blade, so it must be cut with either multiple passes of a saw-blade, routed out with a straight bit, or sawn and chopped out with hand tools.

## Cutting a housing by hand

It is no problem to cut a housing with hand tools, but the process can be very time-consuming and tedious if the components involved are more than 50 mm (2 in) wide.

**1** Begin by laying out saw lines across the width of the board, using a 90-degree T-square set. The distance between the lines equals the thickness of the piece to be fitted into the housing. Also, use a marking gauge to scribe a line indicating how deep you want the groove to be. Generally, housings are about one third to one half the thickness of the stock. Scribe the depth line on both edges of the board, to ensure that the saw-line will end up parallel to the face of the board. To ensure accuracy, deepen the scribe-line with a marking knife and use a chisel to cut a slight trough between the waste section and the knife-line to guide the saw.

**2** Make a saw-cut along each of the layout lines. Remember to split the line and keep the saw on the waste side of the cut in this case towards the section of wood between the two lines. You can cut along the lines freehand, or clamp a guide block along the line to help keep the saw perpendicular to the face of the board.

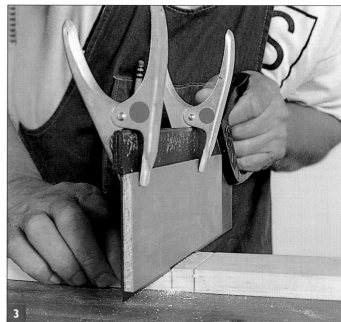

**3** To make it easier to cut all the lines to the same depth, clamp a scrap block to the side of the saw. When the guide block reaches the surface of the board, the saw will no longer cut.

**4** *Chisel out the waste between the two saw marks. For maximum control, work with the bevel of the chisel down. This will avoid the chisel digging too deeply into the wood surface.*

**5** *After chiselling away most of the waste, flatten the bottom of the groove with a chisel. This time work with the bevel up, so that the flat back of the chisel will slide along the bottom of the groove and the bevel will shear away any irregularities.*

**6** *Test fit the joint by inserting the mating piece into the groove. The pieces should fit snugly together, but it should not be necessary to apply much* force. *It may be necessary to pare the sides of the groove slightly, if the pieces will not fit together properly.*

## Alternative Methods

A more common way to cut housings is on the table saw with a special set of blades, called a housing set. The set includes two outer blades, plus a series of cutters and cardboard shims that can be used to adjust the width of the cut. Once the set is mounted on the saw, housings can be cut in a single pass.

If you have just a few housings to cut, you can also mark out the joint and remove the waste with multiple passes over a standard saw-blade, then clear up the cut with a chisel. You can also remove the waste with a router and straight bit.

## SIMPLE REBATE

Rebate joints are based on another type of groove: a step along the edge of the board. They are especially good for creating a recess to accept a plywood back on a bookcase or other case. Once the back is fitted into the recesses a rebate makes a good guide for ensuring that the case is square. Rebates can also be used in drawer-making or for attaching the top shelf to a bookcase, as shown in the drawing. Rebate joints can be fastened with glue or with glue plus nails or screws.

You can construct rebates by making several overlapping cuts with a table-saw, fitted either with a housing set or standard blade, depending upon the width of the rebate. I find it easier to make rebates with intersecting cuts of a standard combination-tooth table-saw blade.

1  *Set the width of the rebate by adjusting the distance between the fence and the outside edge of the blade, then make the first rip cut along the edge of the board. Note how the height of the blade determines the depth of cut.*

2  *To ensure a safe, accurate cut, use push sticks and feather boards to guide the stock, without getting your fingers anywhere near the blade.*

**3** *After adjusting the fence location and blade height, if needed, rip the board again, this time on edge. Set up the fence so that the waste section is on the outside of the blade, not against the fence where it could jam. As an added precaution, do not stand directly behind the blade when ripping, just in case a scrap should catch on a blade tooth and be hurled backwards.*

## Alternative methods

Special planes, equipped with fences and blades designed to cut rebates, are available from major tool suppliers, but they are somewhat expensive. In the interest of speed and economy, many workers opt for routers as a substitute for such planes. You can rout a rebate using special rebating bits with guide bearings that run along the edge of the board or with a regular bit chucked in a router and guided by an auxiliary fence clamped to the workpiece.

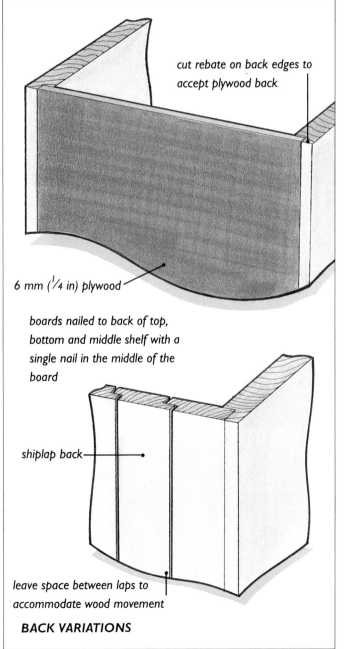

*cut rebate on back edges to accept plywood back*

*6 mm ($^1\!/_4$ in) plywood*

*boards nailed to back of top, bottom and middle shelf with a single nail in the middle of the board*

*shiplap back*

*leave space between laps to accommodate wood movement*

**BACK VARIATIONS**

# DECORATING A SIMPLE BOOKCASE

If you're building a bookcase for your garage or workshop, you probably don't mind if the joints show or if the design is high on utility and low on aesthetic appeal. But you can make it into something decorative with just a few details.

Try concealing the housings by running a narrow strip of moulding down the front of the uprights, or cut simple stopped housings. Because the groove stops about 13 mm (½ in) short of the front edge of the upright and the shelf is notched, the joint is difficult to see.

You can also shape the overhanging edge of the bookcase's top shelf or cover its edges with moulding, too. Alternatively, try running a mitred frame with scalloped edges around the top and base of the case.

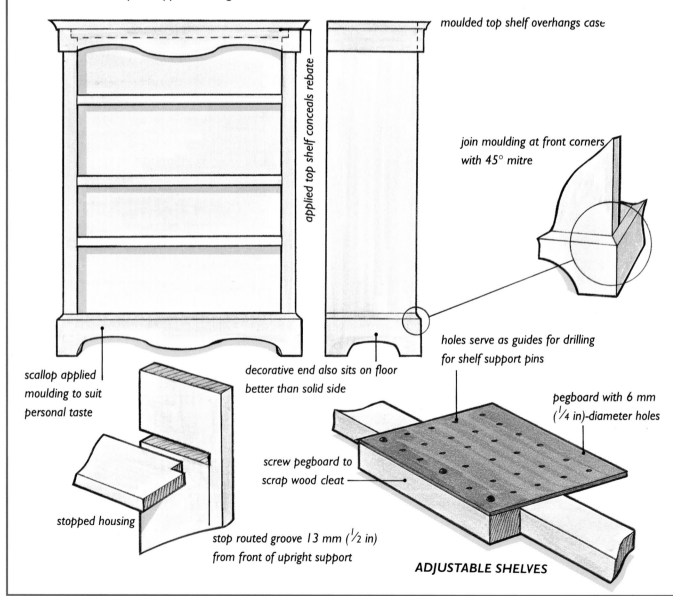

*applied top shelf conceals rebate*

*moulded top shelf overhangs case*

*join moulding at front corners with 45° mitre*

*holes serve as guides for drilling for shelf support pins*

*scallop applied moulding to suit personal taste*

*decorative end also sits on floor better than solid side*

*pegboard with 6 mm (¼ in)-diameter holes*

*screw pegboard to scrap wood cleat*

*stopped housing*

*stop routed groove 13 mm (½ in) from front of upright support*

**ADJUSTABLE SHELVES**

# Picture Frames

The mitre is one of woodworking's most common joints. It is found on cupboard doors, tops of chests and other places where two pieces join at a right angle and where you do not want the end grain of the pieces to show. Since the mitre does not have any interlocking parts, the joint is not by itself very strong and it is not usually used for any structural work. The joint can be reinforced with a dowel or spline.

Most picture frames are based on 45-degree mitres at the corners, or you can work with other angles to create speciality frames that are octagonal (eight-sided) or some other shape. In either case, the principles of cutting the joint are the same, only the angles and number of components change.

**I** *Clamp a mitre box to your bench or work surface. You can make your own box, or buy a variety of fixed and adjustable boxes. The adjustable boxes, like the one shown, can cut to the right or the left and be set at any angle from 0 degrees to 45 degrees.*

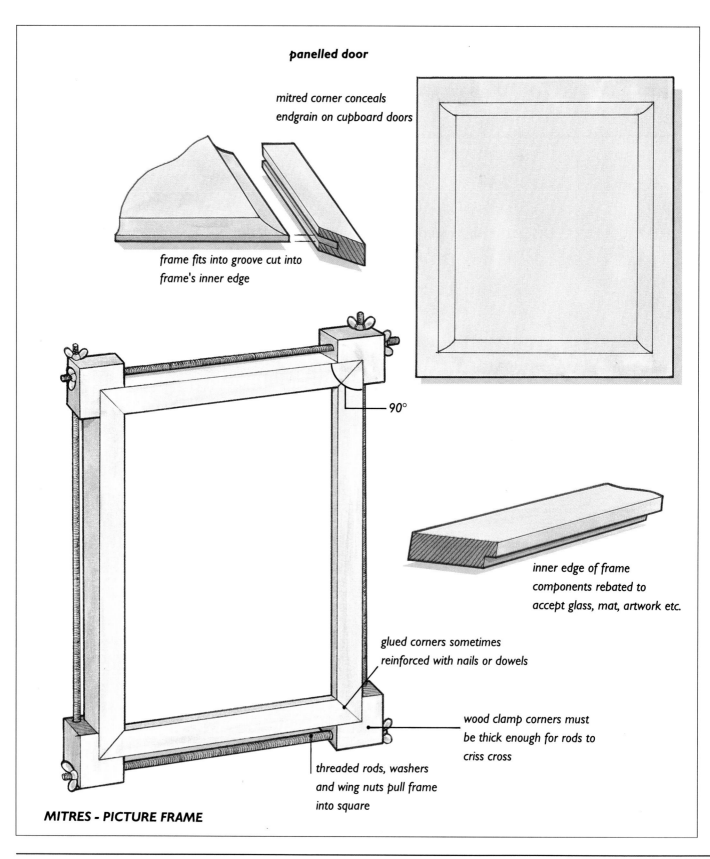

**panelled door**

mitred corner conceals
endgrain on cupboard doors

frame fits into groove cut into
frame's inner edge

90°

inner edge of frame
components rebated to
accept glass, mat, artwork etc.

glued corners sometimes
reinforced with nails or dowels

wood clamp corners must
be thick enough for rods to
criss cross

threaded rods, washers
and wing nuts pull frame
into square

**MITRES - PICTURE FRAME**

**2** *Set your mitre box to 45 degrees, and make the first cut. Remember you lose some of the length because of the section lost in the angle itself, so be sure to adjust your measurements when you rough-cut the components. Reset the box to the other side and repeat the process to cut the next corner.*

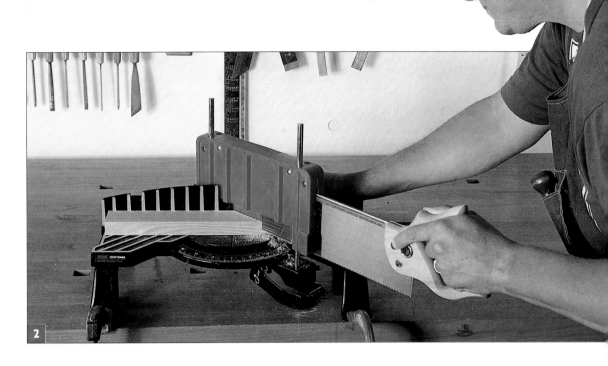

**3** *Mitre boxes can also be used for other jobs, in addition to cutting frame stock. They are ideal for making very accurate 90-degree cuts across boards.*

**4** *Some woodworkers take advantage of this feature to cut tenon shoulders. You can also cut moulding and wider compartments on edge.*

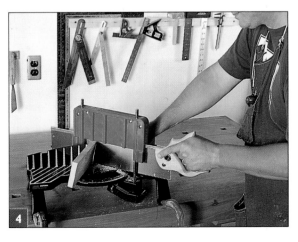

## CHECKING FOR SQUARE

A simple way to check if a frame or box is square is to measure the diagonals, from corner to corner.

If everything is square, the diagonals should be equal in all directions. If not, realign the pieces slightly until the measurements are identical. If you have the piece clamped up, it may be necessary to readjust or remount the clamps.

# Simple Boxes

*Boxes are wonderful projects in their own right, and a basic component for many furniture pieces. A chest of drawers, for example, is basically a box with special supports to house drawers, which are themselves a type of box.*

The simplest way to make a box is to cut four pieces to length, butt the ends together and fasten them in place with glue and nails or screws. Nail on a plywood bottom, perhaps a couple of hinges and a top and you have a serviceable box. I make many boxes like this for simple storage in the workshop.

These boxes are not terribly elegant, however, and the butt joint is not the strongest one available. It can be difficult sometimes to align slippery, glue-covered ends as you try to nail or screw the pieces together. A better approach is a joint like the rebate and tongue that offers more glue surface than the butt joint, and has a mechanical part that helps to align the pieces. As we will see with dovetails, these mechanical locks can be very decorative in some cases.

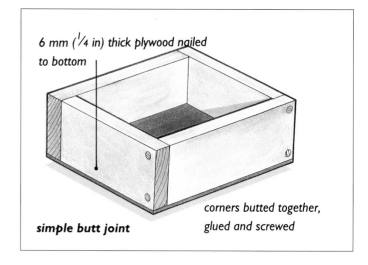

6 mm (¼ in) thick plywood nailed to bottom

**simple butt joint**

corners butted together, glued and screwed

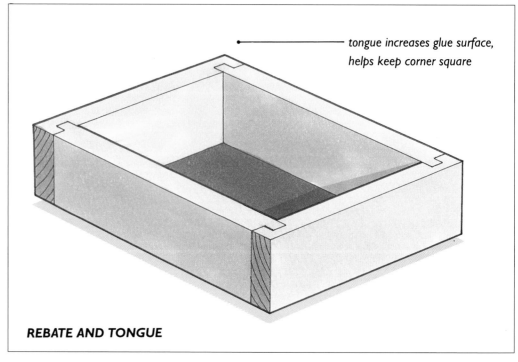

tongue increases glue surface, helps keep corner square

**REBATE AND TONGUE**

# REBATE AND TONGUE

The rebate and tongue joint works well on small boxes, shelves and the backs of drawers, where its ability to help square up the unit is a real advantage. You can cut the joint with a saw and chisel or a router, using the same techniques as for housings, but the table-saw method is faster and more efficient.

**1** Set up the table-saw, so that the distance between the fence and the outside face of the blade equals the thickness of the pieces to be joined. Set the blade height to cut about a quarter to one-fifth of the thickness of the stock, butt the end of the stock against the fence and cross-cut the piece, using the mitre gauge to guide the stock.

**2** Hold the mating piece against the end of the board you have just cut and mark the thickness of the tongue on a scrap piece with a sharp pencil. For most small boxes, the thickness of the blade is fine for sizing the groove and consequently the tongue. For larger set-ups, do not make the tongue thicker than a quarter the thickness of the stock.

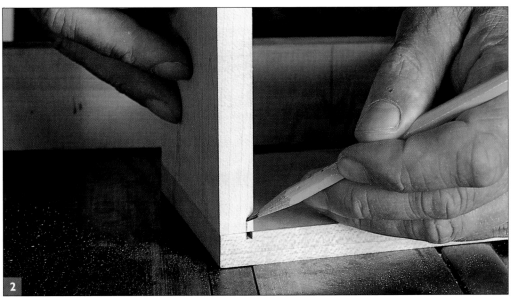

**3** Hold the scrap on end against the fence and adjust the fence as needed to cut a groove along the side of the marked-out tongue. Do not change the height of the blade. Cut across the end, again using the mitre gauge to support the piece. If the stock is long you may need to screw a high, auxiliary fence for added support. Check the fit of the tongue and adjust the fence as needed.

**4** To cut the waste, place the tongue board flat on the saw table, with the tongue on the top of the piece, and raise the blade to cut out the section beneath the tongue. Push the end of the tongue against the fence, and cross-cut.

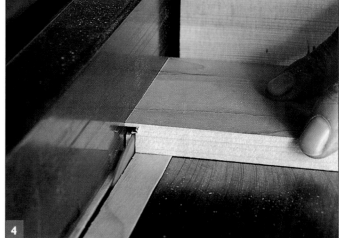

## Variations

The tongue and rebate can be used in places other than the end of the board. For shelves, for example, it is often less obtrusive than a full-thickness housing. It is also useful for installing dividers in knick-knack shelves.

**5** To assemble the joint, simply push the tongue into the groove.

# SPLINED MITRE

The splined mitre is very similar to the mitres cut for picture frames, but this time the joint is reinforced with a spline, a thin strip of wood that both helps to align the piece and greatly increases the glue surface and strength of the joint.

The joint is effective in both solid wood and plywood. With solid wood, though, you must be aware of the grain direction of the components and spline to avoid wood movement problems. The grain direction of the spline must follow the grain of the pieces being joined. This is not a problem with plywood. One problem with the joint, which might discourage you from using it when working with larger components, is that all the corners must be clamped together simultaneously.

The table-saw with a tilting arbor is ideal for cutting splined mitres.

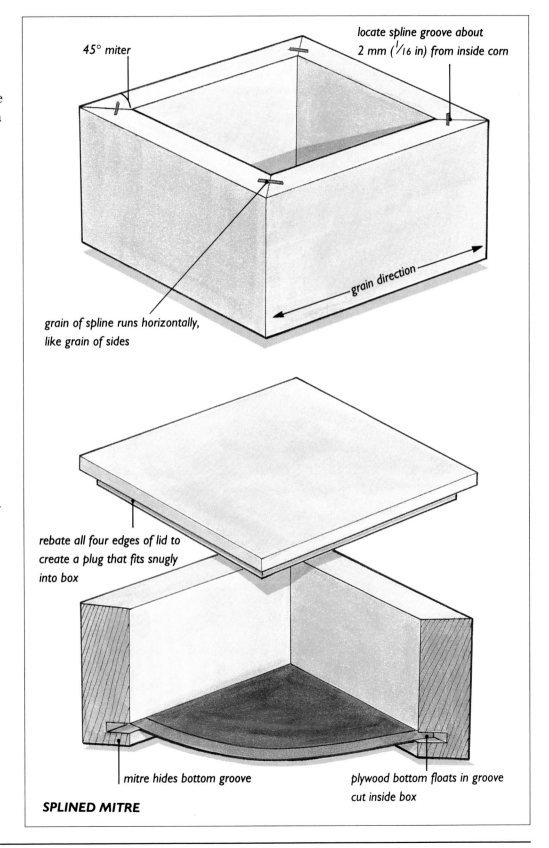

45° miter

locate spline groove about 2 mm (¹⁄₁₆ in) from inside corn

grain direction

grain of spline runs horizontally, like grain of sides

rebate all four edges of lid to create a plug that fits snugly into box

mitre hides bottom groove

plywood bottom floats in groove cut inside box

**SPLINED MITRE**

1 Tilt the saw-blade to a 45-degree angle. The angle scales on most saws are inaccurate, so I use a draftsman's 45-degree angle to set the blade initially. Cut a piece of scrap in half, mate the ends and check the angle with a T-square. If it is not a perfect 90 degrees, adjust the blade again and repeat the test until perfect.

2 Once the blade is set, cross-cut the ends of the mating pieces. Again, use a mitre gauge to support the stock during the cut.

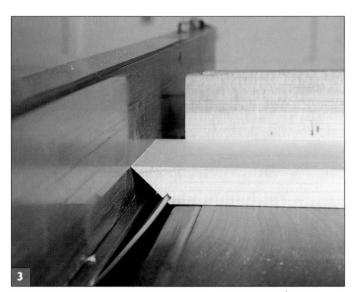

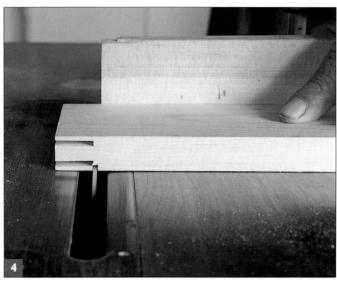

**3** After cutting all the mitres, proceed to cut the slots for the splines. Move the fence to the side of the blade opposite the direction of the angled teeth. Then lower the blade height, so that the spline slot will be cut about one-fifth of the way in from the inside corner. With a 19 mm ($\frac{3}{4}$ in) thick piece, leave about 2 mm ($\frac{1}{16}$ in) between the edge and spline. A 3 mm ($\frac{1}{8}$ in) thick spline is fine for small boxes. Cut the groove with the end of the board running against the fence.

**4** When cutting the spline remember that the grain of the spline must match the grain of piece to be joined to avoid cross-grain constructions. Cut this in two passes, just as with the tongue and rebate. Cut into the end of the piece to establish the thickness of the spline, then put that face-down on the table and cross-cut again to free the spline. For plywood constructions, use a snug-fitting strip of plywood for the spline.

**5** Clamp up the corners with sash clamps, band clamps or specially designed corner clamps, which support both pieces at the corner, and hold them together until the glue dries.

# DOVETAILS

Cutting dovetails is much like learning to ride a bicycle. At first you will not understand how it is possible, then one day you will find you are just doing it and wondering what the fuss was all about. Though there are certainly easier-to-cut joints, the dovetail is worth learning. Dovetails have long been considered by many to be the epitome of craftsmanship. Once you get the hang of the dovetail, the whole process is rather soothing and relaxing.

There are several types of dovetails, but we shall concentrate on through dovetails, which present a distinctive design look because of the dovetail shapes created by the alternating pattern of tails and pins at the corner of a piece. Generally, the tails are about twice as large as the pins.

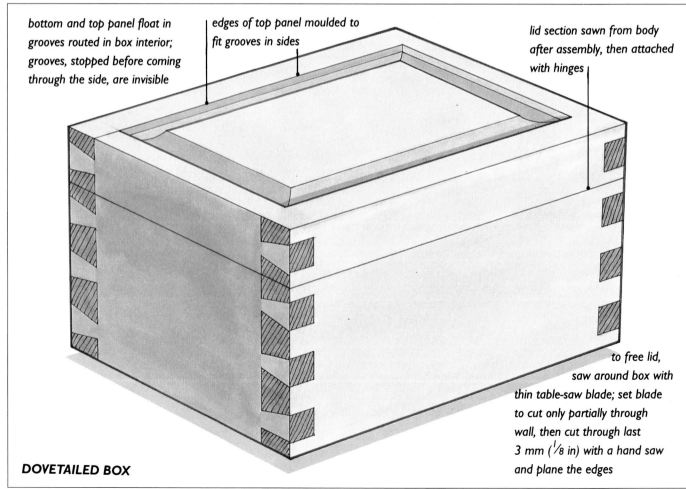

*bottom and top panel float in grooves routed in box interior; grooves, stopped before coming through the side, are invisible*

*edges of top panel moulded to fit grooves in sides*

*lid section sawn from body after assembly, then attached with hinges*

*to free lid, saw around box with thin table-saw blade; set blade to cut only partially through wall, then cut through last 3 mm ($^1/_8$ in) with a hand saw and plane the edges*

**DOVETAILED BOX**

**1** *After cutting the components to size and double checking that all the edges are square, lay out the joint with a marking gauge. Set the gauge to the thickness of the wood, plus about 0.5 mm (¹⁄₆₄ in) extra. The extra length makes it easier to assemble the joint and get a good fit, and can be sanded off after assembly. Draw lines on all four faces.*

**2** *Now lay out the joint on the end grain. Woodworkers argue about whether to do the pins or the tails first, but I learned from a man who thought it was easier to do the pins first.*

*The spacing of the pins varies with the width of the wood. You can choose any arrangement that appeals to your eye. In marking out, start by putting the base of the* gauge on the face of the board and using the angled tongue to lay out the half-pins, the outermost pin on each side. The name comes from the fact that they are angled on only one side, not that they are half the size of the others.

**3** *To help visualize the difference between pins and tails, remember tails are drawn straight across the end grain with a T-square, whereas the end grain lines on a pin board are angled with a bevel gauge, so pins are evenly spaced with their wider ends towards the inside face of the board.*

**4** *After laying out the end-grain lines, use a T-square to carry the lines down each face of the board to the scribed depth line you previously made. Once you have more experience you will do this by eye.*

**5** *It is always confusing in the beginning to remember which part of the joint is waste. Make sure you mark the waste clearly.*

**6** *Saw down the lines with a back saw or dovetail saw. The finer the better. Use your thumb as guide to keep saw to waste side of the line, following or splitting the line. Do not saw below the scribed line.*

**7** *After sawing out the pins, you are ready to chop out the waste with chisel and mallet. Before doing this, however, put some scrap wood under your work to protect your bench and use a chisel to cut the marking gauge line deeper. Widening the layout line creates a little trough that will help to ensure a straight cut all the way across the board. Make a V-cut at the back of the line, so that the chisel can rest up against it.*

## SETTING ANGLES WITH A BEVEL GAUGE

When woodworkers talk about dovetail angles they often refer to a 1:6 ratio for softwoods and a 1:8 ratio for hardwoods. You can measure the angles, but a quicker way is just to mark out the ratios and set your bevel gauge.

Draw a square line across a piece of wood. Divide the line into 150 or 200 mm (6 or 8 in) increments, using a ruler or a compass. Mark a point 25 mm (1in) from the line, along the edge of the board.

After connecting that point with the 150 or 200 mm (6 or 8 in) mark on the line across the piece, put the base of a sliding bevel against the edge. The lower part of the tongue should be on the 25 mm (1 in) mark on the edge of the board and the other end on the 150 or 200 mm (6 or 8 in) mark on the line. Lock the gauge and transfer the angle to the board being joined.

**8** *Use a chisel to remove most of the waste. Chisel only halfway down from each face, so you do not tear out fibres as you cut through the end grain. The back of the joint should be undercut slightly to ensure a tight fit. Clean out corners, if necessary.*

**9** *Scribe the tails from the pins. Use a sharp awl and mark from the inside of the pieces. Place the tail board on the bench and hold the pin board on it. The angle of the pins will help force the awl point against the pins. Carry square lines across the end grain, if you like, and remove the waste with a chisel as before, except that you are cutting out the opposite section.*

**10** *All the sections can be undercut, except for the spaces on the end that will accept the half-pins. Undercutting would show here. Instead, mark off square lines and saw off the end pieces.*

**11** *Before assembly, test fit all pieces and trim as needed. Put a little glue on the pins and push the pin board into the tail board. It may be necessary to use a block of wood and mallet to push the pieces together, but be careful to avoid breakage.*

# Carcases

*Case pieces are found in every home and office, and can take many forms – desks, bureaux, display units, music centres and other types of free-standing or built-in cabinet.*

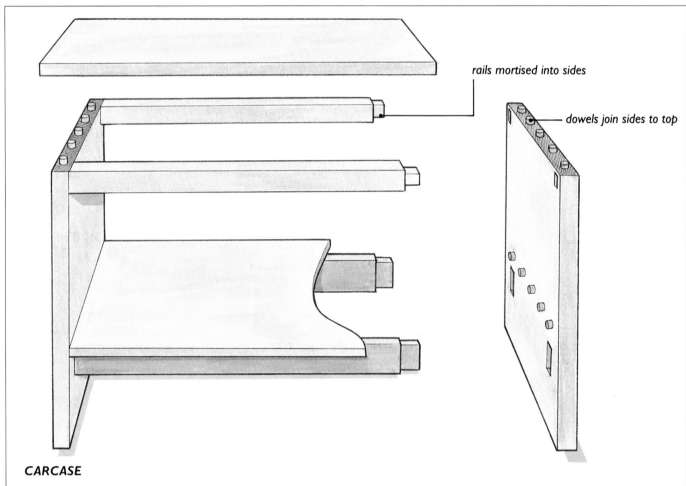

rails mortised into sides

dowels join sides to top

**CARCASE**

Early cabinetmakers often built these case pieces using wide boards, but they frequently cracked because of cross-grain constructions and wood-movement problems. Modern workers avoid the cross-grain constructions and often substitute frames assembled from fairly narrow components for large slabs. The frames are grooved on their inner edges to accept thin panels. There is enough space between the panels and frames to allow the panels to expand and contract with seasonal humidity changes.

Two of the most common joints used to form frames and join other carcase components are the dowel and the mortice and tenon. Both systems can be used in the same case, as shown in the diagram.

# DOWELLING

Dowels have always been a favourite of mine. The joint is invisible, so it does not interfere with the clean lines of a piece plus, it is easy to do. You drill mating holes in the two pieces, glue in a small wooden pin and push everything together. As long as the holes are square and true and the mating edges properly milled, everything comes out OK. There are many dowelling guides on the market to make sure those holes are properly drilled. These guides feature clamp-like devices that lock on the wood and support a guide block sized to accommodate various sizes of drill bit.

Of course, some woodworkers frown on dowel joints as not being very strong. Certainly a mortice and tenon is a stronger joint, and avoids many of the end-grain gluing weaknesses, but the joint is strong enough for most applications. The furniture industry certainly uses a lot of them. I once asked a restoration specialist about the strength of dowels, imagining he had seen many joints that had failed. He estimated that the joint typically was good for 40 years. After that, he said, it might loosen up, but it was easy to reglue.

If you buy a dowelling jig, get one that is self-centring. For most jobs the dowel is centred in the thickness of the wood, so it is easier to let the gauge handle that aspect. If you want something offset, you can always add a shim to one side of the gauge. Also if you want to put a dowel in the middle of a piece too wide for the dowelling guide to grasp, simply use the guide to make your own gauge. Take a piece of squared-up stock that will fit in the gauge, drill guide holes as needed, then locate the block on the board where you need to bore holes.

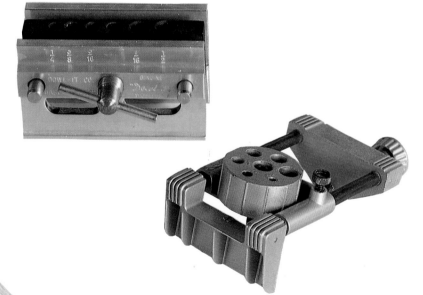

*Choose a dowelling jig which is sturdy and well-made.*

**1** Lay out the joint by drawing lines where you want to locate dowels. For accuracy, I put the joint together, then draw the lines across both pieces simultaneously.

**3** Adjust the depth of cut by inserting a drill bit through the jig block and gauging it against the dowel. The holes in each mating piece should be a little more than half the length of the dowel. An extra 3 mm ($\frac{1}{8}$ in) or so of space is needed to accommodate any excess glue.

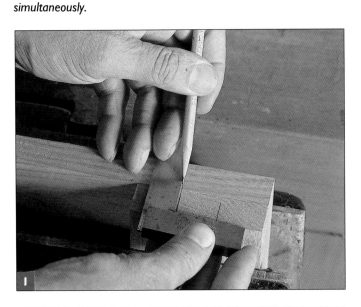

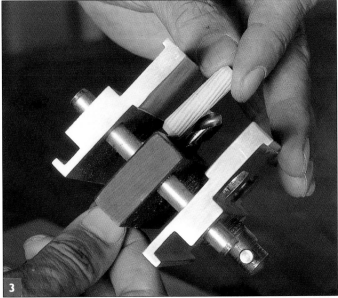

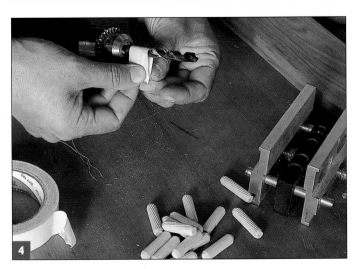

**2** Locate the dowelling jig on your layout line. Note that the guide block has holes for several sizes of drills and an alignment mark for each size. Locate the mark for the dowel/drill size you are using, in this case, 9 mm ($\frac{3}{8}$ in) diameter, on the layout line. Depending on the design of your jig, you may have to carry the layout lines to another face for proper alignment.

**4** Mark the depth of cut with a masking-tape flag, so that all the holes will be bored to the same depth.

**5** Secure your work in a vice and bore out the hole with the bit in a portable electric drill. Bore the hole until the tape flag reaches the surface of the drill block.

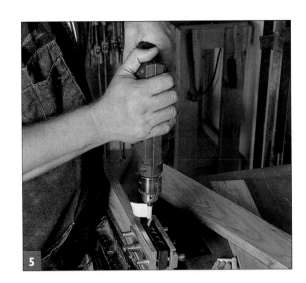

**6** Add glue to the holes. I always put a coat of glue on the mating surfaces, even though the end grain does not make the best glue joint, but it makes me feel better.

**7** Insert the dowels. It will probably be necessary to tap them in with a mallet or hammer.

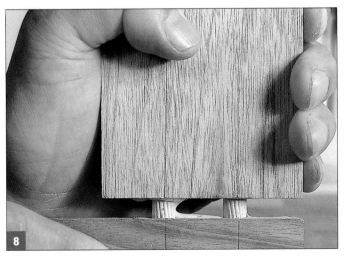

**8** Put glue in the mating holes and fit the joint together. Clamp until glue dries.

## Alternative method

**1** Another handy way to make dowel joints is with dowel points. They come in sets of pairs for holes ranging from 6 mm ($\frac{1}{4}$ in) diameter to 13 mm ($\frac{1}{2}$ in).

Drill holes in one piece and put dowel centres in the holes. It is important that the holes be straight and square, so use a drill press, if possible, or use a T-square to help you align the drill.

**2** Once the dowel centres are inserted, push that piece up against its mate, being sure to align the two properly.

**3** The dowel centres will mark dimples on the surface that have to be bored. The best bit here would be a brad point or lip and spur drill, which has a centre pin or screw point to help align the bit and keep it from skipping across the surface. Again, take care in aligning the drill and use a tape flag to ensure the hole is bored to proper depth.

# MORTICE AND TENON JOINT

The mortice and tenon is a very strong joint and one of the essential elements of any woodworker's arsenal. This joint excels at supporting weights from above and keeping things square. It is used for frame-and-panel sides for carcases (see diagram), leg and aprons for table bases, leg and rails for chairs and other items.

The strength of the joint comes from the large glue surface between the cheeks of the tenon and the walls of the mortice that house it. In both cases the glue bonds side grain to side grain. In addition, the shoulders of the tenon hold everything square and resist twisting.

Generally the tenon is cut on the horizontal pieces, called rails, and the mortice is cut in the verticals, called stiles. The tenon should be about one-third the thickness of the stock. Avoid trying to cut four shoulders because it is difficult to get them on the same plane and reduces glue surface, thereby weakening the joint.

You can make a mortice and tenon with a variety of hand and power tools. With most methods layout is very important. Generally the mortice is made first, because it is the harder part to cut, then the tenon is sized to fit. It is far easier to trim the cheeks of the tenon with a sharp chisel than it is to cut into the walls of a mortice.

*A mortice and tenon joint has a large surface area for gluing and so is very strong.*

**1** Lay out both the mortice and tenon with a morticing gauge. This gauge cuts both lines of the mortice or tenon at once, so it is much more accurate than using two settings with a standard marking gauge. Again, when marking out either the mortice or the tenon, work from the same face of each piece.

**3** You can chop out the mortice entirely with chisels. Mortice chisels, which are heavier than standard butt chisels, are designed for this job, but it is easier to bore out most of the waste on a drill press. Use a bit that is slightly narrower than the desired mortice. Drill the end holes first, then eliminate the waste working in toward the centre. This ensures accuracy on the ends of the mortice. The drill bit can wander on subsequent cuts, when it will not always be supported on all sides. Use a tape flag on the drill bit to judge the depth of cut. If you do not have a drill press, you can bore the holes freehand or use a dowelling jig to align the bit.

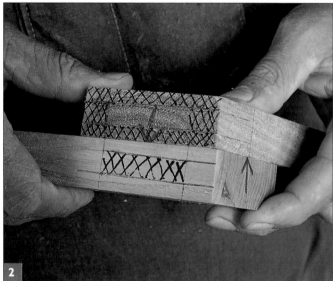

**2** Marking out the waste with a pen is not usually necessary, but it does give a good idea of the mechanics of the joint and the cutting and chopping operations that are required.

**4** *After boring out most of the waste, clear out the remaining waste and pare to the layout lines with a chisel.*

**5** Tenons can be cut in a variety of ways. The important point to remember is that the shoulders should be square and in the same plane on all faces and that the tenon fits snugly into the mortice.

**6** Remove the waste by cross-cutting on the table-saw. Set a stop block on a fence to ensure all the shoulder cuts will be the same. Butt the stock against the block, clamp or hold it snug against the mitre gauge and advance the stock into the blade. The tenon is not actually in contact with the block during the cut, so the little waste scrap slides safely away, without being trapped between the fence and blade and possibly being thrown back.

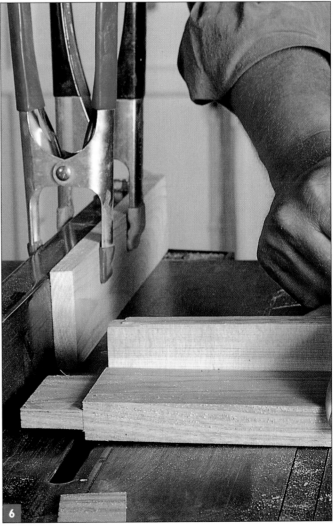

**7** *Repeat the operation with the stock on edge, to remove the top edge of the tenon. Again, butt the piece against the fence and block assembly before starting the cut, to ensure the shoulders are all cut the same.*

**8** *You can remove the remaining waste on a bandsaw or by making multiple cuts on the table-saw. Overlap the cuts to remove waste.*

**9** *Pare with a chisel until the tenon fits. Use the back of the chisel as a guide to ensure a flat, clean cut. Be careful not to pare it out of square.*

## Alternative Method

A plunge router is a good tool for quickly cutting accurate mortices.

**1** *Attach a fence to the router, and screw a piece of wood to the fence. The piece should be at least 25 mm (1 in) wider than the length of bit, so that it contacts the stock before the bit does. With the fence tight against the work and the bit over the mortice location, plunge the spinning cutter into the wood and cut back and forth until the desired depth is reached. The bit diameter sets the width of the mortice. The stops on the plunge router control the depth of cut. Rout the whole mortice, then stop the tool before removing the bit.*

**2** *If the mortice piece is too narrow to work with the fence on your router, sandwich the workpiece between two pieces of squared-up scrap. You can rout the width of the mortice by hand, or you could mount stops on the assembly to prevent the cut from extending beyond the layout lines.*

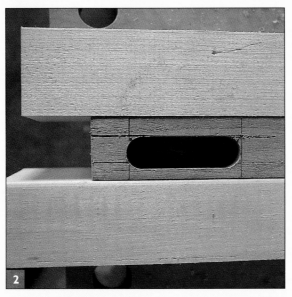

**3** *Since the router bit leaves a mortice with round walls at the ends, you either have to square up the corners with a chisel or round over the corners of the tenon. It is easier to round the tenon. Just turn over the edge with a rasp or file, then refine the corner with a piece of sandpaper, using the same motion you would to polish shoes with a cloth.*

# Doors

Doors use a variety of joints. Heavier exterior doors rely on large haunched mortises or double mortise and tenons. The haunch, a little horn on top of the tenon, fits in the grooves used to mount panels in the door. In addition to filling the hole, the haunch also helps prevent the door from twisting. Smaller doors also use mortise and tenons and joints like the half-lap.

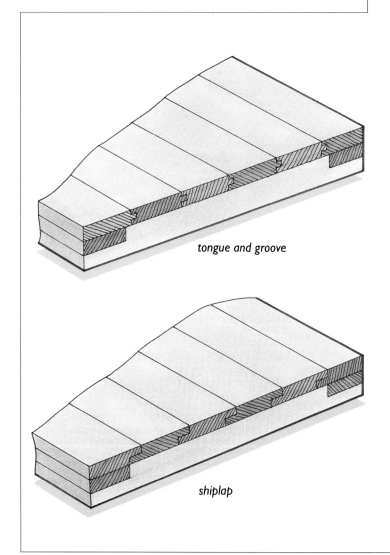

tongue and groove

shiplap

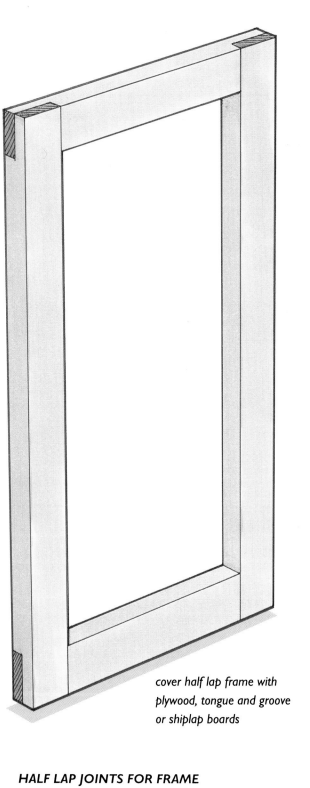

cover half lap frame with plywood, tongue and groove or shiplap boards

**HALF LAP JOINTS FOR FRAME**

# THE HALF-LAP

The half-lap is just what its name implies – you remove half the thickness of each component, then lap the two pieces together, so that the resulting joint is the same thickness as one of the original components.

The joint has a great deal of glue surface, but it is not as strong as a mortice and tenon, which it resembles. Generally, lap joints are employed for cabinet work, doors, and other non-structural work. It can also be used as a design accent, since it contrasts end grain against side grain, as on this vividly figured Southern Pine piece (below).

You can cut the joint with any of the methods used to cut housings or tenons. Basically, all that is involved is removing the waste, then paring to fit.

You can also cut the joint with a router, or use the router to clean up the surface after roughly sawing away the waste.

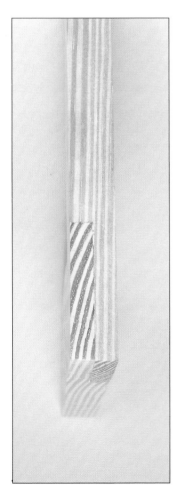

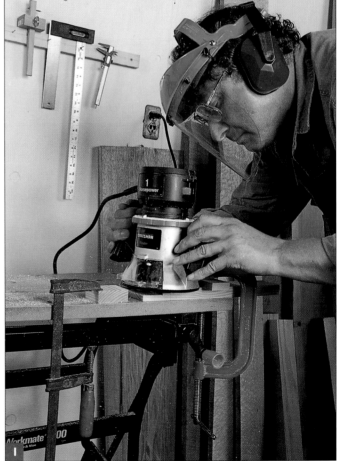

**1** *To rout out the lap joint, you need a straight bit and a guide fence.*

**2** To locate the fence, determine the distance between the cutting edge of the router bit and the edge of the router base. This distance will vary according to the diameter of router bit being used, so it is a good idea to check your measurement before each job, unless you always use the same router and bit set-up. After marking out the shoulders of the joint, locate the fence to guide the router. To do this measure off a space back from the shoulder that equals the distance between the router base edge and the bit. Draw a straight, perpendicular line across the board as a guide for setting the fence. It is important that the fence be mounted exactly perpendicular to the edge of the workpiece.

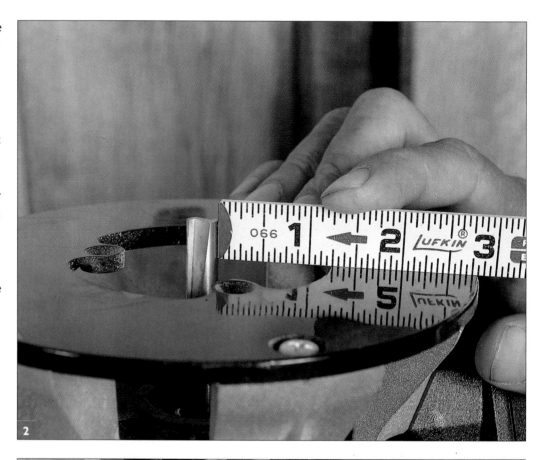

**3** If you are working on the end of the board, it is very hard to support the router on the edge, so mount an auxiliary board in front of the workpiece to support the router at the beginning of the cut.

**4** *Remove the waste in stages, starting on the end of the board and moving toward the fence. Work slowly, always moving the router so that the bit is rotating toward the surface being cut. If you move with the rotation, the router could pull itself away with a dangerous lurch. The same method can be used to remove waste in the middle of a board; just mount a fence on each side of the joint.*

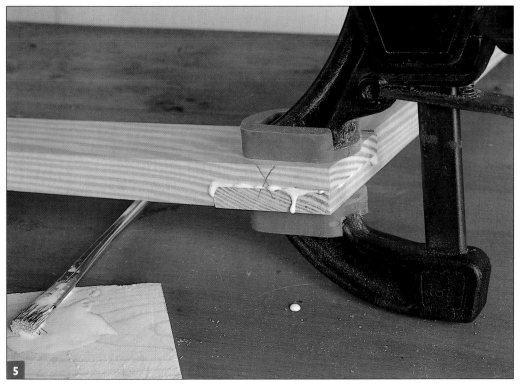

**5** *When you assemble the joint, you must clamp the two laps together to ensure a tight joint.*

## Alternative Method

A router table is a good way to clear away waste or trim tenons and half-laps. You can hold the piece flat on the table or rig some type of clamp to hold it down.

## QUICK REPAIRS

When you are getting ready to assemble a project, you might find a sliver has come up along an edge of a board. Rather than try to cut this off, you can sometimes make an invisible repair by working a little glue into the opening. A toothpick or thin-bladed knife works well for inserting the glue. You can also use a needle and syringe.

After inserting the glue, clamp the sliver in place with masking tape. Hook the tape on one side of the board and stretch it tightly over the sliver. Hold the sliver down as much as you can when you do this. Let the glue dry for several hours and sand away any residue.

You can also repair minor cracks and secure loose knots with cyanoacrylate adhesive, which is sold under various trade names as instant glue. One brand comes in several consistencies, along with a catalyst to speed the curing process. Be very careful with this stuff – it will bond skin as well as wood. Just squirt a little of the clear, thin consistency grade into the crack and let it cure. Do not use the catalyst. The glue will bubble up and turn white when the catalyst hits it and the repair will be very noticeable. This does not usually happen if you just let the glue cure on its own.

Also, if you have to fill a crack you can sometimes make a good patch by sanding the surface and working the sawdust into the opening. When the crack is filled with sawdust, squirt on some instant glue and let it cure before sanding the surface again.

*Above: Work a little glue under the sliver.*

*Above: Fix the glued sliver with masking tape.*

# HAUNCHED MORTICE AND TENON

Haunched mortice and tenons are often found on doors, especially panelled ones. In addition to moving the tenon away from the edge of the board and filling the groove, the haunch makes it easier to cut the panel grooves, because you do not have to worry about stopping them short of the end of the board. Just machine the groove all the way to the end and fill it later with the haunch.

Follow whatever procedure you choose for making the tenon. The tenon is generally as thick as the panel groove is wide. The haunch must be long enough to fill the groove. In many cases, it turns out to be just about as long as the tenon is thick.

When working with doors and similar pieces, it is very easy to tear out the top wall of the mortice while inserting the tenon and haunch. To avoid this, the rails are usually allowed to run an inch or so long, to create horns on the top of the piece. These horns are trimmed after assembly.

haunched tenon for panelled door

**PANELLED DOOR**

# WORKING WITH WOOD GLUES

The strength of most joints lies in how well the components fit together, not in the amount of glue that is used. Large amounts of glue can't compensate for poor workmanship; it may actually make the problem worse. Most woodworkers rely on PVA (Polyvinyl Acetate) or aliphatic resin glue. PVA is usually white and takes longer to dry than the aliphatic resin, which is usually yellow. Both glues dry relatively clear, so glue lines are virtually invisible if the joint is well cut.

When you glue the long edges of several boards to make a table top or other large panel, you can end up with lots of glue on the surface if you are not careful. I generally put a thin coat of glue on each edge, although some workers coat only one edge in each joint. Then I clamp everything together, using bar or sash clamps. Locate the clamps about 300 to 600 mm (12 to 24 in) apart, and alternate them on the top and bottom

of the assembly to keep everything flat. Sometimes you also have to put a piece of scrap wood across the panel and use a hammer to re-position any boards that might have slipped in the glue.

Every dot of glue on the surface must be removed before a finish can be applied. The best way to do this is to scrape the glue off with a chisel or putty knife when it starts to get gooey. Some people wash it off with a wet cloth, but that often just spreads a thin layer of dilute glue over everything.

Let the glue dry overnight and scrape or sand away any remaining residue. If you miss a bit of glue, the finish will appear as a white spot or smear in that area. Usually you have to remove the glue with a chisel or sandpaper and reapply the finish. It is a lot easier to clean it off in the first place.

*Leave panel in clamps for at least 30-60 minutes with yellow glue, longer with white glue. Check glue manufacturer's recommendations.*

*Tighten clamps to pull pieces together and produce a thin bead of glue.*

*Over-tightening clamps can force out most of the glue, starving the joint and creating a weak joint.*

*Pressure from clamps spreads out in a fan-like pattern.*

*Alternate clamps, top and bottom, to keep panel flat.*

*If edge of panel won't be trimmed off, pad clamps with scrap wood, to avoid damage to edge.*

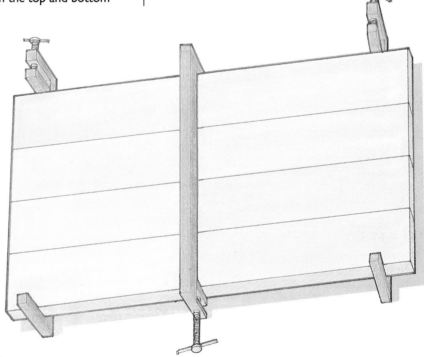

**CLAMPING PANELS**

# BOARD AND BATTEN DOORS

Board and batten doors are the familiar barn doors many of us, at least in rural areas, enjoyed swinging on when we were youngsters. They were often a little creaky and certainly not airtight, but the braces holding them together made great perches for the adventurous.

These doors can be made in a variety of sizes, from barn door to shutter.

Generally, they are used where an airtight seal is unnecessary. In many older houses I have seen them on cupboards, especially built-in ones. And residents in urban areas fit them on enclosures designed to keep pests away from rubbish receptacles. It is possible to make the board and batten door airtight if you wish, by sandwiching insulation and/or a vapour barrier between two layers of vertical boards.

Sometimes an outside frame is also added to dress up the edges.

A typical board and batten door is built with just a few easily assembled components: a series of relatively narrow boards, 50–100 mm (2–4 in) wide, running vertically, with their edges butted together, and secured by two or three horizontal battens. In addition, a brace is run diagonally across the door to keep everything square and prevent sagging when the door is hung on hinges. The brace is usually notched into the cross battens, but sometimes the brace is simply butted against the batten. Battens and braces are usually about the same width as the vertical components, or slightly narrower.

Early doors of this type were often secured by nails, driven all the way through both vertical boards and battens and brace. The protruding points of the nails were then clinched over with a punch, for the protection of anyone running into the door and to make the nails snug. Most newer doors are held together with screws that run through the brace and battens into, but not through, the vertical boards. To avoid wood movement problems, the screws are mounted in slots. As the vertical boards expand and contract with the seasons, the screws can slide slightly in the slots.

*Above: Working out the position of the battens.*

## SIZING UP BOARDS

When ripping the vertical boards, leave them an inch or two longer than the desired height of the door. It is a lot easier to trim the top and bottom of the assembled door, than to try to align everything perfectly before you attach the battens. Because the end pieces are secured firmly to the batten, though, you can generally get the width of the door right with out too much fuss. It is often awkward to rip the edges of an entire door.

hinges mounted on the side, nearest low end of brace

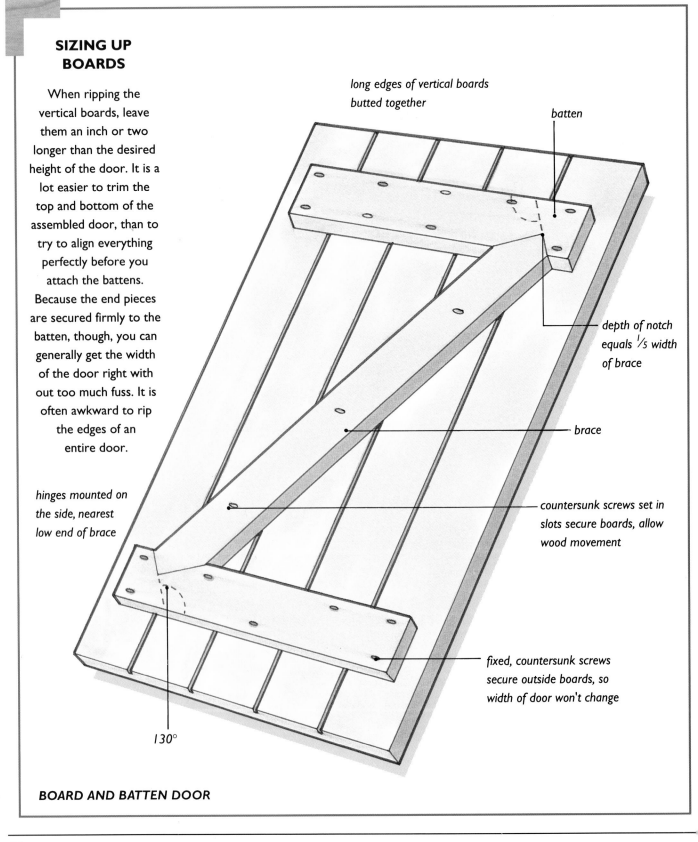

long edges of vertical boards butted together

batten

depth of notch equals $\frac{1}{5}$ width of brace

brace

countersunk screws set in slots secure boards, allow wood movement

fixed, countersunk screws secure outside boards, so width of door won't change

130°

**BOARD AND BATTEN DOOR**

**1**  *After arranging the boards in a way that suits you, clamp everything together to double check the width. To make it easier to rearrange the pieces in the right order, mark them with a large triangle as shown.*

**2**  *While you have the boards clamped, you can also size the battens. Generally, leave about 50 mm (2 in) on each side, so that the door will have enough clearance to swing open or shut without the batten hanging up on the door frame.*

**4**  *Before screwing down the battens and brace, put them in place on the door and lay out the angles on the ends of the batten, as shown in the diagram (page 96). The diagonal brace should be set so that the lower end is on the side of the hinges. The top end faces the free end of the door. First, angle the ends with a sabre saw...*

**3**  *Now is also a good time to take a carpenter's framing square and mark guide lines for mounting the battens.*

**5** *...Then, use the brace ends as patterns for tracing the corresponding notches in the battens. I have cut the notch with a sabre saw, but you could use any hand saw or a bandsaw, if you have one.*

**6** *Next, drill screw holes through the battens and brace. All the holes are elongated, except for the two outermost holes on the end of each batten, which must be fixed to ensure that the width of the door will not change after assembly. For the elongated ones drill two or three holes together with a hand-held power drill. I use a bit that both cuts a pilot hole, sized slightly larger than the screws, and countersinks the area around the hole. That way the installed screw sits slightly under the surface of the door, yet is still free to move in the notch to accommodate seasonal changes.*

**7** *Remove the waste between the holes with a saw, chisel or file.*

**8** *Put the components in place on the door, then make a pencil mark at each screw location. That way you can make sure that each board is secured with at least a couple of screws. Begin assembly by screwing down the battens at the ends. Once these screws are fixed, all seasonal wood movement is accommodated by the boards between the two outside verticals.*

**9** *After securing the batten ends, put a screw in each slot.*

**10** *Then trim the top and bottom of the door to size with a sabre saw or hand-held circular saw. To make the door easier on the hands and prevent sharp edges from chipping, round over the outside edges slightly with a hand plane or pad sander.*

# TONGUE AND GROOVE DOORS

Tongue and groove doors are very similar to board and batten doors, but are more airtight, since a tongue cut on the long edge of each vertical board fits snugly into the groove cut into the edge of the adjacent board. Each board has a tongue on one side and a groove on the other. Boards on the outside edges of each door are ripped to remove the tongue or groove and create a solid edge.

Because the tongues fit into the grooves, there are no open spaces between the components, as with the board and batten. If the boards expand and contract, the movement is not usually sufficient to pull the tongue out of the groove or force it against the bottom of the groove, causing a break.

Since seasonal humidity changes do not cause openings in tongue and groove panels, it is often applied to create backs for bookcases or other carcases. In these instances, a decorative bead may be cut down the edges of the board along the joint.

The tongues and grooves along the edges of a board can be cut with a router, shaper or table-saw fitted with either a moulding head with matching cutters, a standard housing head or saw-blades. I find the table-saw method works well, without forcing an investment in additional equipment. I cut the groove with a housing head, then cut the tongue with a double-saw blade set-up.

Since I find it easier to trim tongues than to expand grooves, I always cut the grooves first, then size the tongue to fit it. Generally, it works out to having the tongue about one third to one quarter the thickness of the wood.

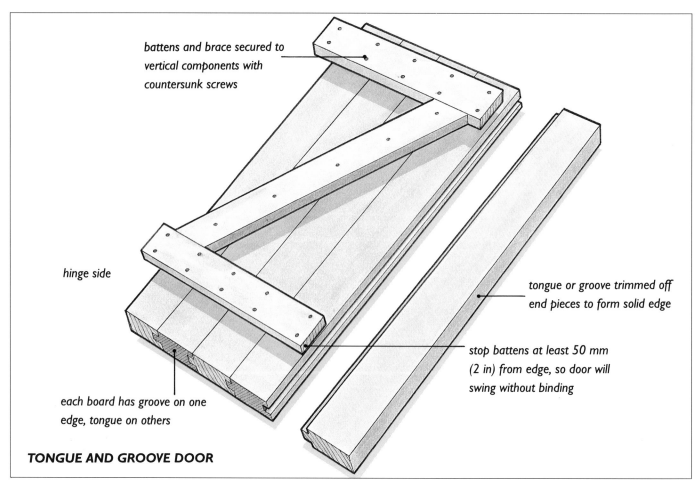

battens and brace secured to vertical components with countersunk screws

hinge side

each board has groove on one edge, tongue on others

tongue or groove trimmed off end pieces to form solid edge

stop battens at least 50 mm (2 in) from edge, so door will swing without binding

**TONGUE AND GROOVE DOOR**

1 To cut the grooves, set up the tables as shown in the photograph. The width of the housing, in this case formed by two cutters, determines the width of the groove. The depth of cut is set by lowering or raising the blade assembly on the table-saw. Adjust the distance between the fence and the blade to centre the groove on the edge of the board.

2 Use a similar set-up to cut the sides of the tongue, but this time mount two saw-blades on the saw arbor at the same time. The width of the tongue is set by adding spacers between the blades. For this set-up I made a washer with 6 mm (¹/4 in) thick plywood, then added a thin cardboard and a paper shim. Do not forget to account for the set of the saw teeth when installing the spaces. On most blades the teeth lean slightly away from the flat face of the blade.

3 After cutting the side of the tongue, all that remains is to remove the thin sliver of waste on each face. Use a single blade and set it to just cut through the thin waste strip. A push stick is used to move the stock over the blade. The waste strip falls away as the board is pushed off the saw.

**4** *If, when you slot tongue into groove, it is a little tighter than the desired gentle piston fit, plane each edge slightly with a rebate plane. It is an easy operation, because this plane has a cutter that is exactly flush with its sides. Set the blade for a fine cut. Rest it with the plane body against the edge of the stock and sole on the side of the tongue and push gently. Thin shavings can be removed until a proper fit is achieved. Mine is a Japanese-style wooden plane, but other models are available.*

**5** *After fitting the tongues in the grooves, add a clamp to pull everything tight, then drill countersunk holes to secure the assembly with screws. I put at least one screw in the centre of each board.*

**6** *Once the battens are secure, place the brace in position, diagonally across the door, and mark where it intersects with the battens.*

Since these pieces were only slightly wider than the standard table-saw fence, I did not have to install a taller auxiliary fence to do this cut. If the boards are wide and there is a danger of tipping, install a higher fence, and install feather boards as previously described, to help guide the wood through the cut.

As with any joinery involving the table-saw, be careful. In the case of the tongue and groove joints, not much material is removed, but still ensure that the hand holding the stock against the fence and down on the table is well behind the blade and that the fingers of your trailing hand, which are pushing the wood, are only on the top corner of the piece.

**7** *Connect the points facing each other to determine the angle for cutting the brace to fit between the battens. As an option, you could notch the brace and battens, as on a board and batten door (see page 98).*

**8** *Then, trim the door to size on a table-saw – which is appropriate for a small door like this. On a larger, more unwieldy assembly, use a handsaw or hand-held power saw.*

**9** *Finally, round the sharp edges with an electric-powered pad sander.*

# Drawers

Drawers are nothing more than boxes with a purpose. First, they offer very convenient ways to store everything from pins to tools safely out of view since the drawers are designed to slide in and out. Drawers can be made in a variety of sizes, although in designing a drawer it is a good idea to relate its size to the kind of material being stored. A drawer for shirts can be larger than one for storing tools, without interfering with ease of use.

In addition to practical considerations, drawers also can be decorative. They visually break up the front of a case, and can be accented with inlay, thin strips of contrasting wood let into grooves cut in the drawer front, moulding, handles and knobs. Knobs can be turned or carved from wood, if you like, but many workers select commercially available brass, pewter or glass ones.

Most of the techniques for box-making can be applied to drawers: dovetails, rebates and housings are commonly seen. Rather than repeat what we have said about these joints and techniques, though, let us look at some of the special modifications that make a drawer different from a box.

The drawer shown in the drawing is very simple. The front is rebated on all four sides to create a lip around the perimeter of the front. The bottom of the front is also grooved, as are the sides, to accept a 6 mm (¼ in)-thick plywood bottom. The back just fits between the sides and this butt joint is secured with nails and glue.

The front of a drawer is generally cut from 19 mm (¾ in)-thick stock. It can be sized to fit flush with the front of the carcase. This requires fairly precise fitting, so you might prefer to start with the lipped drawers shown. The lip also prevents the drawer from being inserted too far into the opening and hitting the back of the case.

If you do not have a lip on the drawer, you will probably have to mount a stop, just a wooden block

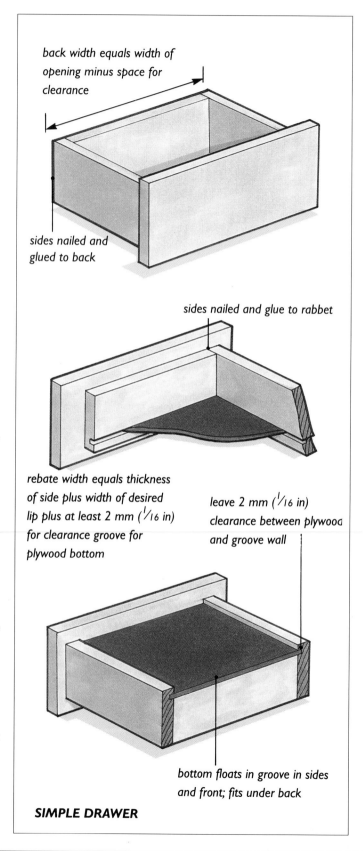

back width equals width of opening minus space for clearance

sides nailed and glued to back

sides nailed and glue to rabbet

rebate width equals thickness of side plus width of desired lip plus at least 2 mm (¹⁄₁₆ in) for clearance groove for plywood bottom

leave 2 mm (¹⁄₁₆ in) clearance between plywood and groove wall

bottom floats in groove in sides and front; fits under back

**SIMPLE DRAWER**

screwed to whatever kind of drawer support you use. The back of the drawer hits the stop before it can be pushed in too far.

Drawers should fit snugly into the opening, but must make some allowance for wood movement. There should be at least a 2 mm ($\frac{1}{16}$ in) of clearance all around. Some American woodworkers follow the old adage of leaving a space the thickness of a dime (2 mm/$\frac{1}{16}$ in) in damp weather and the thickness of a nickel (3 mm/$\frac{1}{8}$ in) in drier weather to compensate for seasonal wood movements.

For flush drawers, the rebate should equal the thickness of a side plus about 2 mm ($\frac{1}{16}$ in), to give you a little room for final fittings and adjustments. For lipped drawers, the rebate equals the width of the desired lip plus the thickness of a side, plus 2 mm ($\frac{1}{16}$ in) or so for clearance.

The sides of the drawer are not seen most of the time, so they are generally made from plywood or a lesser grade of wood than the fronts. Poplar is a good wood for drawer sides. Generally, sides are 13 to 16 mm ($\frac{1}{2}$ to $\frac{5}{8}$ in) thick, although sometimes thicker stock is used when the sides are grooved to fit on runners fastened to the walls of the carcase. These drawers are called side hung.

The sides are cut to fit snugly in the drawer opening, then hand-planed to allow free movement. Often the top edges are slightly rounded over, to make the sides a little easier on the eyes and the touch.

The back is also made of a secondary wood, such as 13 mm ($\frac{1}{2}$ in) thick plywood or poplar. The back can be grooved to accept the bottom or sized so that the bottom will slide under it. The bottom is usually of something like 6 mm ($\frac{1}{4}$ in) plywood. If the bottom fits in grooves, it is usually cut to leave about 2 mm ($\frac{1}{16}$ in) play all around. If the bottom is to be nailed to the back, it generally extends a little bit beyond the back.

Some variations on ways to mount drawers are shown in the drawing. Side-hung drawers are fairly easy for beginners. Simply cut a 16 mm ($\frac{5}{8}$ in) wide groove into the side of the drawer, then mount a guide onto the side of the case. The drawer will slide smoothly back and forth on the guide.

Other supports include a frame housed or dowelled into the side. These frames, which are often fitted with a plywood dust panel, provide a solid bottom for the drawer and are often found on high-quality work. You can also fasten a channel guide to the bottom of the drawer and mount a runner from front to back in the case or mount an L-shaped runner on each side. The L-shaped runner can be machined from a single piece or formed by screwing two pieces together.

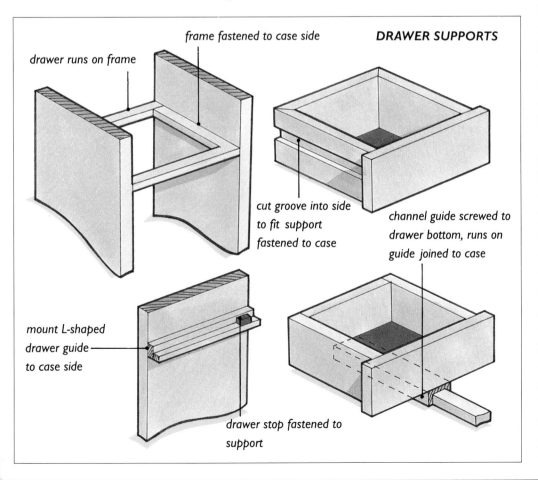

**DRAWER SUPPORTS**

drawer runs on frame

frame fastened to case side

cut groove into side to fit support fastened to case

channel guide screwed to drawer bottom, runs on guide joined to case

mount L-shaped drawer guide to case side

drawer stop fastened to support

# TONGUE AND GROOVE (Router)

The tongue and groove joint is also often used for drawers. The joint is actually very similar to the tongue and rebate joint used to make a small box in a previous section (page 69), but this time the joint is blind, so its component parts are not readily visible from the front or sides of the drawer. The components are cut with a router and the tongue extends into the

sides of the drawer, so it will resist the forces applied when the drawer is opened and closed.

For the drawer shown here, the front is 22 mm ($^{7}/_{8}$ in) thick butternut and the sides and back are 16 mm ($^{5}/_{8}$ in) thick pine. One groove is cut into each end of the drawer front and one groove is cut into each inside face of the drawer sides.

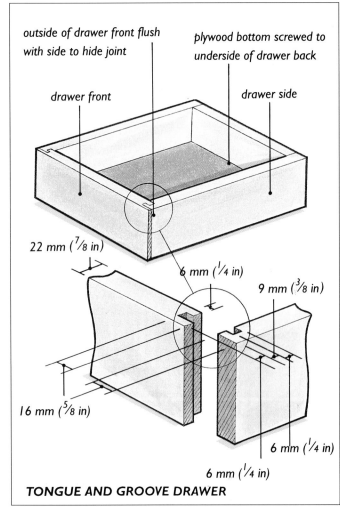

outside of drawer front flush with side to hide joint

plywood bottom screwed to underside of drawer back

drawer front

drawer side

22 mm ($^{7}/_{8}$ in)

6 mm ($^{1}/_{4}$ in)

9 mm ($^{3}/_{8}$ in)

16 mm ($^{5}/_{8}$ in)

6 mm ($^{1}/_{4}$ in)

6 mm ($^{1}/_{4}$ in)

**TONGUE AND GROOVE DRAWER**

**1**

1 In laying out the joint, divide the ends of the drawer front in three sections vertically: a solid section on the drawer front which will overlap the side and hide it from view, a groove to accept the tongue on the drawer side and a 6 mm ($^{1}/_{4}$ in) thick tongue, which will be trimmed back to fit into grooves on the

side pieces. Lay out this section with a T-square. There are no exact guidelines here; you can have a little variation to match the diameters of the bits you have available. I just divided the board up into three sections: 6 mm ($^{1}/_{4}$ in) for the front, 9 mm ($^{3}/_{8}$ in) for the groove and then 6 mm ($^{1}/_{4}$ in) for tongue.

**2** Next, set the front piece against the side, and mark the location of the groove in the side. The fence on a router table can then be adjusted to locate the groove. The distance from the outside of the groove to the end of the side piece equals the thickness of the drawer front minus the overlap.

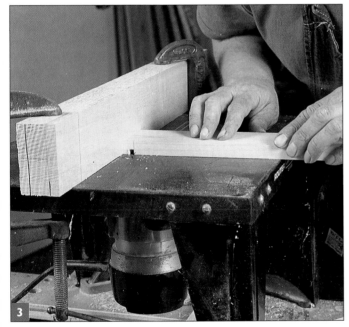

**3** The groove can be cut in a single pass, since it is only 6 mm ($\frac{1}{4}$ in) deep. The drawer side is wide enough to provide an adequate bearing surface on the fence, so just push the side against the fence and push it over the bit. Repeat the operation for the second side.

**4** Once the groove is cut put the pieces together to mark out the width of the groove that must be removed from the drawer front 9 mm ($\frac{3}{8}$ in) in this case.

**5** *The depth of cut must equal the thickness of the side, so that the outside face of the side will be flush with the end of the drawer front when the pieces are assembled. Again, rather than measure, put the pieces together and mark the depth needed.*

**7** *The final step is to trim back the length of the 6 mm (¹⁄4 in) tongue on the drawer front, so everything fits together. Trim the ends on the table-saw, or you could do this with a backsaw.*

**6** *To rout the groove in the drawer front, hold the piece on end against the high fence and slowly slide the piece over the bit. You can make the cut in two passes with a 6 mm (¹⁄4 in) bit, shimming the fence with an 3 mm (¹⁄8 in) thick add-on between cuts, or with a single pass of a 9 mm (³⁄8 in) bit.*

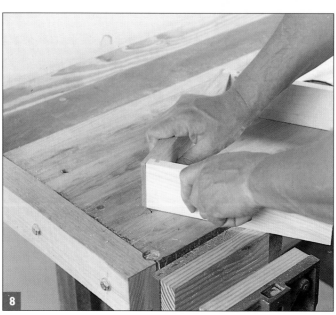

**8** *Double-check everything by test fitting the pieces together.*

# *Tables*

*Although a table might seem too complicated a project for a beginner, the joints used are based on ones you are probably familiar with.*

## LEG AND APRON JOINT

Once you can cut a mortice and tenon joint, you should not have any problem with a leg and apron joint. It is basically the same process,

except usually one of the components is a somewhat thick, square leg and the apron is thinner and more rectangular.

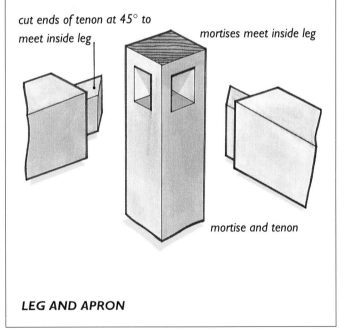

cut ends of tenon at 45° to meet inside leg

mortises meet inside leg

mortise and tenon

**LEG AND APRON**

I  *Mortices are chopped by hand or router, as previously discussed; use whatever method you like.*

2

**2** If the leg is slender, though, you will have to add another step. Cut the end of the tenons at a 45-degree angle so that they will fit together inside the leg where the mortices meet.

**3** Although they are not as strong as a mortice and tenon, you can also use dowels to join aprons to legs. You can also reinforce the joint with wood blocks.

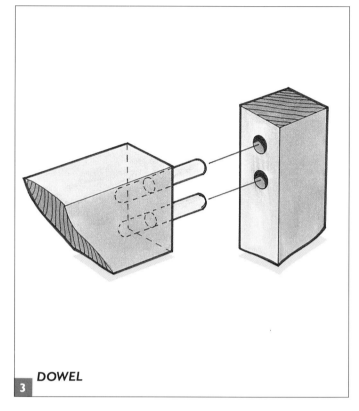

**3** **DOWEL**

## JOINING TOPS TO APRONS

A large, solid wood table top can be extraordinarily beautiful, despite its natural impulses to self-destruct. As we said, wood always moves, so table tops can cause quite a problem for many builders.

There are several ways that you can attach a top and still allow for movement. One is to make traditional cabinet-maker's buttons. These are little blocks of wood with tongues that fit into a groove that runs along the inside edge of the apron. The tongue fits into the groove, then the block is screwed into the top. As the table expands and contracts, the buttons can shift slightly in the grooves. One other caution – a common mistake when installing screws into a top is to be a little careless about the depth of the countersink and the length of a screw. It can be pretty disheartening to see that screw come out through your finely finished top. You can also run screws up through the apron. Put a single screw in the middle of the table at the ends. Either make the holes oversized or mount a hole large enough to allow a washer under the screw to slide with movement.

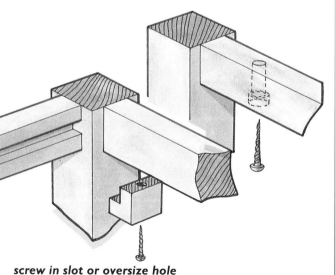

*screw in slot or oversize hole*

# BRIDLE JOINT

The bridle joint or slip joint is much like a topless through-mortice, with the tenon sandwiched between two uprights and exposed at the top and bottom. The joint is fairly strong, because of the surface area, but sometimes it is awkward to clamp the piece in both directions to get the shoulders and cheeks tight.

One other thought – the joint is strongest at the top of a leg, or other location where downward pressure is supported by the bottom of the groove. If you need a joint at the bottom of a leg or some other place where downward pressure would only be resisted by the holding power of the glue, use another joint. Without some sort of mechanical advantage the joint will weaken prematurely in these situations.

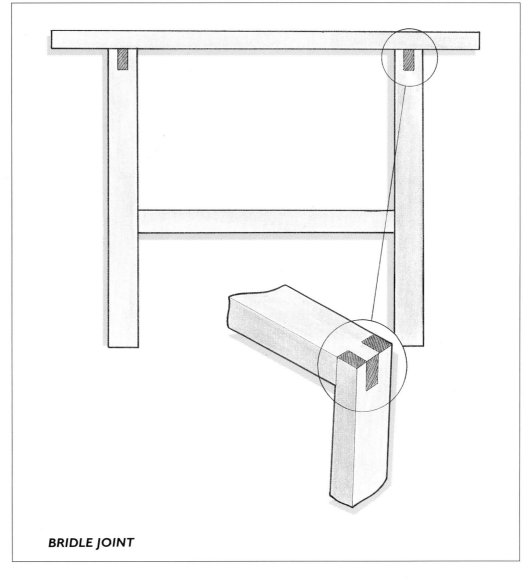

**BRIDLE JOINT**

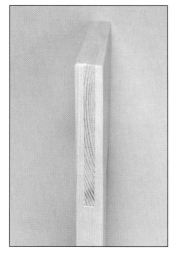

**I** *Put mating pieces together, so you can mark the proper widths for the tenons and open mortices. Use a T-square to ensure accuracy during layout.*

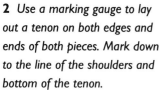

**2** Use a marking gauge to lay out a tenon on both edges and ends of both pieces. Mark down to the line of the shoulders and bottom of the tenon.

**3** Mount each piece in a vise and saw the cheeks. Cut on the waste side of the line. For the tenon, the cuts are on the outside of the line; for the mortice, they are on the inside of the line.

**4** Before cutting the shoulder, deepen the layout line by dragging the edge of the chisel down the line. For maximum chisel control, deepen the line in several passes rather than make one deep cut. Some workers cut a small V to make the guide even more definite.

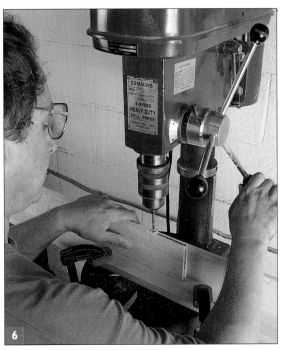

**6** *Chisel out the centre section for the open mortice; work in from both sides. Undercut the bottom, as you did for a dovetail, to ensure a good fit. You can also drill a hole near the bottom of the waste area to make it easier to remove the centre in a large chunk.*

**5** *Fit the backsaw in the groove and cross-cut the shoulder. A bench stop is handy for holding the piece during the cut.*

**7** *Fit the pieces together and clamp.*

## EDGE TREATMENTS

A simple router table set-up is perfect for rounding over the edges of a board or cutting a variety of shapes in wood. The rounding over bit shown (1) has a pilot bearing to guide the wood as it is being cut.

Just feed the board into the direction of the cutter rotation and the bit will do the rest. For the smoothest cut, make at least two passes. You can remove most of the material in the first pass, then make another pass, just taking off a tiny bit to polish up the edge.

The router set-up does not have to be anything fancy. Mine is a small commercially available table that I clamp to a Workmate (2). I use it so often that I keep one router permanently mounted. When I need a fence, I just clamp on a strip of wood.

The set-up can also be used for ploughing grooves and other shapes in the middle of the board. Make sure to use a fence and push sticks (3).

# WEDGED MORTICE AND TENON

Wedges are thin, tapered slips of wood driven into a tenon to expand it snugly against the mortice walls, thus adding strength to the joint. Two types of wedges are commonly found in furniture work.

The first type, called a foxtail wedge, is concealed inside a closed mortice. As you can see in the photograph, the joint looks like any other mortice and tenon. The wedges are inserted into the tenon, then the tenon is inserted into a blind mortice. As the tenon hits the bottom of the mortice, the wedge is driven home, tightening the tenon.

The second type not only strengthens the joint, but adds to the decorative appearance, since the end grain is visible with a through mortice. The wedges can be inserted singly or in pairs. Single wedges are usually inserted in the middle of the tenon; doubles can be inserted in the tenon itself or on either the top or bottom edge.

There are a couple of tricky, even devilish,

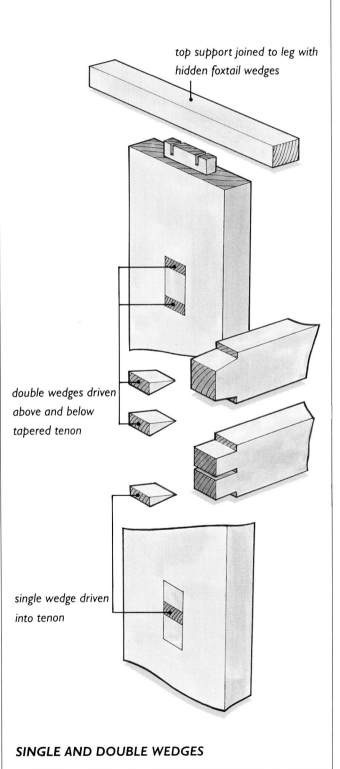

top support joined to leg with hidden foxtail wedges

double wedges driven above and below tapered tenon

single wedge driven into tenon

**SINGLE AND DOUBLE WEDGES**

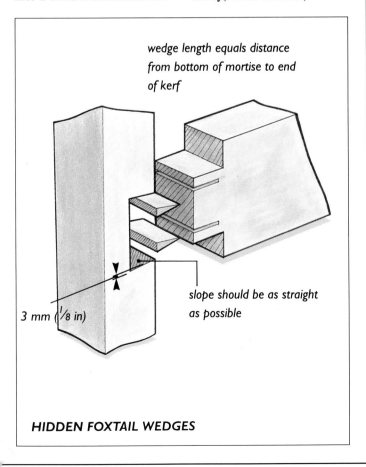

wedge length equals distance from bottom of mortise to end of kerf

3 mm (¹⁄₈ in)

slope should be as straight as possible

**HIDDEN FOXTAIL WEDGES**

aspects of each of these wedged tenons. With both types of mortices you have to expand the end walls so that the wedge-expanded tenon can be accommodated. You also have to be fairly precise sizing the wedges.

If the relationship between the mortice, tenon and wedges are off, the joint will be loose or impossibly tight. This can be a problem particularly with foxtail wedges because everything happens inside the joint during assembly and you do not have much latitude for final adjustments. Many woodworkers avoid the joint altogether.

This is not such a problem with through wedged tenons, because you can see how much space is available and adjust a mortice or tenon where necessary. Also you can let everything run long, within reason, then trim the protruding tenon and wedge after assembly.

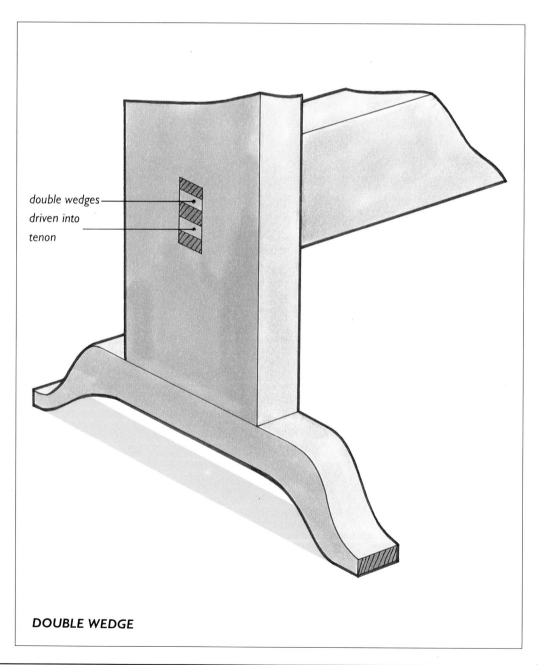

double wedges driven into tenon

**DOUBLE WEDGE**

width of kerf cut in tenon

3 mm (¹⁄₈ in)

grain

depth of saw kerf plus
9 mm (³⁄₈ in)

**1** The techniques and tools for cutting a wedged mortice and tenon are the same as those for cutting standard closed and open mortice and tenon joints. Again cut the mortice first, then the tenon. As you chop out the closed mortice, make the end walls slope back toward the bottom in a straight line. This takes some patient work with a very sharp chisel or gouge. End grain, in particular, does not respond well to dull tools. A file sometimes works well to smooth out rough spots, and makes a good straight edge for checking that there are no humps along the slope.

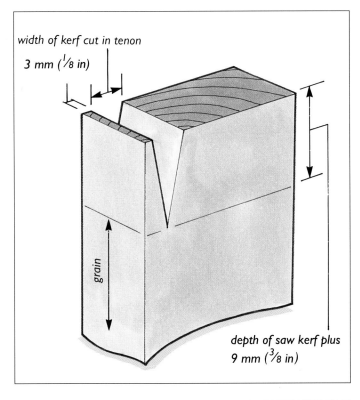

**2** The major modification required on the tenon involves sawing a kerf or two down the end grain, to provide a way for the wedge to enter. Mark the kerf depth, so that it stops about 6 mm (¹⁄₄ in) short of the tenon shoulder.

**3** To minimize chances that the kerf will split farther as the wedge is inserted, drill a small hole, with a diameter slightly larger than the width of the kerf, at the end of the slot.

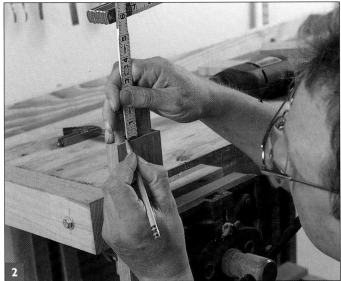

**4** Draw the kerf lines across the end grain with a T-square. The distance between the kerf and the edge of the tenon depends on the flexibility of the wood. On average, the distance will be about 3 mm ($\frac{1}{8}$ in), but you will probably have to experiment a little here.

**5** Next, saw down to the bored hole with a backsaw.

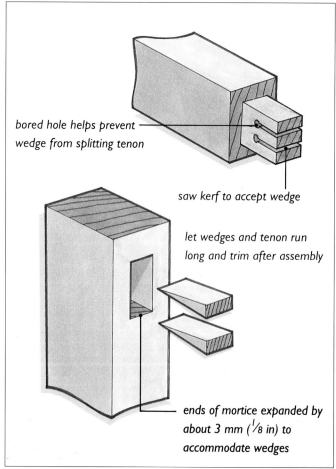

bored hole helps prevent wedge from splitting tenon

saw kerf to accept wedge

let wedges and tenon run long and trim after assembly

ends of mortice expanded by about 3 mm ($\frac{1}{8}$ in) to accommodate wedges

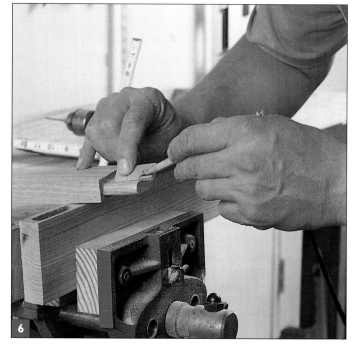

**6** General guidelines for making wedges are shown in the drawings. It is important that they are the same thickness as the tenons. Gauge the length carefully for the closed mortices, so that the wedge will be just long enough to go from the bottom of the mortice to the end of the kerf. If the wedge is too long, it might prevent the joint from closing.

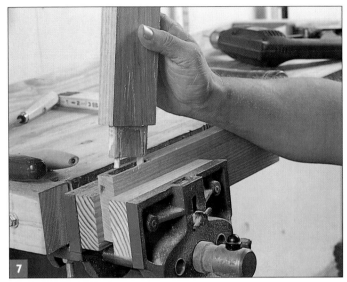

**7** Cover the tenon with glue and insert it into the kerf. Tap them slightly to seat them firmly in the groove, then insert the tenon into the mortice. A clamp will probably be needed to fit everything snugly. In this case the vise supports the walls, but you would be wise to clamp the sides as well as the top of the mortice, if it is close to the end of the piece. This prevents the wedging action from breaking out a chunk of wood.

**8** The procedures for through wedged tenons are very similar, except that it is easier to see what you are doing when you slope the walls of the mortice.

**9** The opening must be expanded by about 3 mm ($\frac{1}{8}$ in), and again, the wall should slope smoothly all the way through the mortice. Check your progress with a T-square tongue or ruler.

**10** Cover the tenon and wedges with glue. Drive the wedges into the kerfs with a hammer. Alternate the blows from wedge to wedge, so that the tenon expands evenly. Continue until the tenon fills the mortice completely (see diagram page 115) then trim the wedges.

Another option, should you not want to expand the mortice, is to taper the ends of the tenon slightly, then drive wedges between the tenon and the mortice.

# TUSK TENON

A tusk tenon is a long through tenon that is secured with a removable, tusk-like wedge. The wedge is a very visible part of the design of the joint. This lets you disassemble the joint quickly and easily; maneuvering a 6ft.-long trestle table up a winding stairway can be a real chore, unless you can disassemble the trestles, unscrew the top and move everything in easily managed pieces.

The same type of tusk tenon arrangement can be applied to other designs, as well as tables. I especially like them on small benches. Alternatively, you could dress up your carpenter's tool box by using a pair of tenons and small tusk tenons to secure each end of the box to the sides. The tusk tenons can also be used instead of bed bolts to secure the rails supporting a mattress to a head board and foot board.

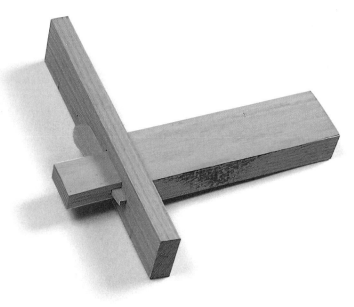

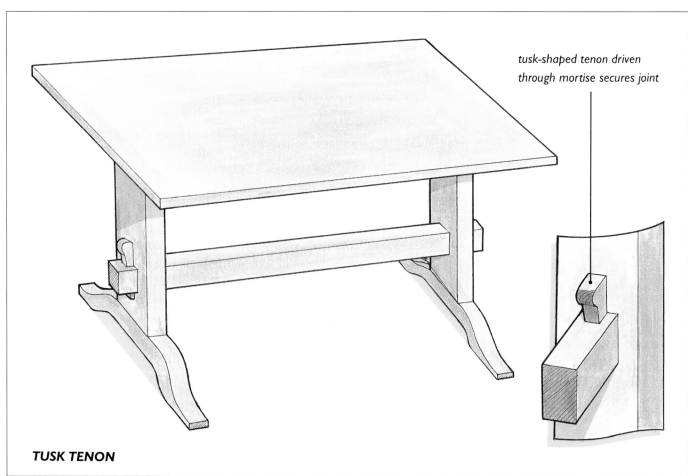

tusk-shaped tenon driven through mortise secures joint

**TUSK TENON**

Making a tusk tenon joint is very much like making any other through tenon. The parts just tend to be a little heavier, especially for pieces that will be subjected to heavy use. Also, you have to cut a mortice with one angled side through the tenon to accept the wedge. The end of the mortice is offset slightly, about 3 to 6 mm (⅛ to ¼ in), inside the member through which it passes. The result of a tapered wedge being driven through a tapered, offset mortice is to pull all the pieces tightly together. If the joint should loosen, you can tighten it by driving the wedge a little deeper into the mortice.

It is sometimes recommended to relieve the top and bottom edges of the mortice which receives the tenon, to prevent the tenon from tearing out the mortice edges as it is inserted and removed, or as it shifts due to seasonal wood movement.

**1** *After cutting the through mortice and tenon, insert the tenon through the mortice and mark where the face of the upright member meets the tenon.*

**2** *Then with a T-square draw a line about 3 mm (⅛ in) closer to the shoulders of the tenon. This line will mark out the straight wall of the tenon.*

**3** *The angled line setting out the other end of the mortice is set with a bevel gauge. Generally a slope of 1:6 or 1:8 is adequate.*

**4** *Before chopping out the wedge mortice, drill a couple of holes through the tenon, then clear the remaining waste with a chisel. The holes go all the way through on the straight wall of the mortice, only partially down on the angled side.*

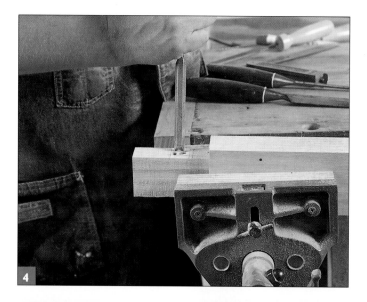

**5** *As you chisel the angled side, line up the chisel with the guide lines on the outside of the tenon.*

**6** *Borrow a trick from plane makers and work in a keyhole saw around the angled wall.*

**7** *Rough spots can be removed with a file. The goal is to make the sloping side as straight and smooth as possible.*

**8** *Wedges can be sawn from the same wood as the tenon or from a contrasting wood. Set the angle of the wedge with the same marking gauge used to lay out the mortice through the tenon.*

**9** *To assemble the joint, put the tenon through the mortice, put the wedge into the mortice and drive it home with a hammer.*

# Glossary

**Across the grain**
At 90 degrees to the grain direction of the wood. On most boards, this would be across the width of the piece.

**Annual rings**
Concentric rings formed under the bark of growing trees in temperate zones. Tropical trees grow constantly, so growth rings are not generally visible. The lighter section of each ring is called spring or early wood, because it is formed at the beginning of the growing season. Darker sections are called late wood or autumn wood.

**Against the grain**
Cutting in a direction that forces the wood to split along the direction of the grain downwards into the wood.

**Apron**
A narrow strip of wood, sometimes shaped, that runs horizontally under a table top.

**Auger bit**
A long twist drill held in a brace for boring holes by hand.

**Bark pocket**
A timber defect caused by wood growing around a chunk of bark.

**Birds' eyes**
Small circular patterns in the wood surface that resemble birds' eyes and that are caused by conical depressions; found in maple and other woods.

**Block plane**
A small metal plane useful for trimming and grain and edges. Unlike the setup on larger planes, the cutter is inserted bevel-up in the body.

**Book matched**
A board sliced in half through its thickness, and then joined together so that the back of the top section mirrors the top of the bottom section, like the pages of a book. This match can also be made with consecutive sheets of veneer sliced from the same tree.

**Brad point drill**
Metal bit with a centre point to prevent the bit from skipping across the wood when starting a hole.

**Burl**
A highly figured section of wood or veneer cut from an abnormal growth that develops on the trunks of some trees.

**Chamfer**
A flat, angled surface, often 45 degrees, planed or carved on the edge of a board.

**Check**
A long, generally shallow split along the length of the board, often caused by improper drying procedures.

**Clean** or **Clear Stock**
Timber free of defects, such as knots.

**Coarse grain**
Wood with wide, visible growth rings.

**Countersinking**
Enlarging the upper part of a bored hole so a screw head can be set beneath the surface of the wood.

**Cove**
A concave, quarter round profile carved or routed on a board's edge or piece of moulding.

**Cross-cut**
Sawing a board across its width or grain.

**Cross grain construction**
Any construction where a long-grain section of wood is fastened securely across the grain of another piece, thereby restricting seasonal wood movement and forcing the piece to crack or twist.

**End grain**
Grain section at a right angle to the length of the board.

**Face side**
The reference side from which all other surfaces are dimensioned.

**Figure**
The decorative pattern visible on a wood surface, which is caused by grain, colour variations, branch growth, injury, interlocked fibres, growth stresses, or other factors.

**Fine grain**
Wood, usually slow-growing, with narrow, fairly inconspicuous growth rings.

**Firsts and seconds (F.A.S.)**
A classification of hardwoods indicating the highest quality pieces.

**Forstner bit**
A metal bit without a lead screw designed to bore flat bottom holes.

**Fruit wood**
Cabinet wood from fruit trees such as cherry.

**Green wood**
Freshly cut timber that has not been dried.

**Grain**
The pattern visible on the wood surface, which is due to the growth rings and the angle at which the board was sliced from the tree.

**Hardwood**
Timber from a tree with broad leaves (deciduous) that are usually shed in the autumn.

**Heartwood**
The darker section of wood extending from the centre of the tree, the pith, to the sapwood.

**Housing**
A square bottom trough cut across the grain of a piece of wood.

**Kerf**
Width of groove left by a saw-blade.

**Kiln-dried**
Wood dried with artificial heat in a large oven-like structure called a kiln. Wood dried without the application of artificial heat is termed air-dried.

**Knot**
Section of branch embedded in a board. Dark, loose knots are generally referred to as dead knots.

**Marking gauge**
A guide block and beam arrangement supporting a small metal point that is used to scribe lines at a set distance from an edge.

**Moisture content**
The amount of moisture present in wood, expressed as a percentage. Generally air-dried wood is about 14 to 15 per cent moisture; kiln-dried lumber about 8 to 10 per cent. Moisture levels change constantly in response to changes in the relative humidity of environment.

**Moisture gauge**
Similar to marking gauge, but the beam has two adjustable points, so that it can mark out both walls of mortice with a single setting.

**Nail set**
A group of metal punches of various diameters, used to force heads of nails beneath surface of wood.

**Ogee**
S-shaped profile combining both concave and convex curves.

**Rebate**
A recess or step cut along the edge of a board.

**Rail**
The horizontal component of a frame.

**Ripping**
Sawing down the length of a board, with the grain.

**Sapwood**
Growing wood section near the outside of the tree. This is usually a lighter colour than the heartwood.

*Continued on next page*

### Scraper
A small, flexible piece of steel that can be sharpened to make a shearing finish.

### Shake
A split between adjacent layers of wood fibres, usually caused by growth stresses or improper drying.

### Softwood
Timber from needle-leafed trees, usually evergreens (conifers) that bear their seeds in cones.

### Spade bits
Paddle-shaped metal bits for boring large holes in wood.

### Spline
A thin piece of wood glued into mating grooves of components to be joined together.

### Stile
The vertical component of a frame.

### Twist drills
Metal drills designed for machinists, but effective for boring small holes in wood.

### Wane
Bark area or missing section along the edge of a board.

### Warping
Distortion of timber, caused by improper seasoning or cutting, or growth factors. The most common forms are bowing, forming a bend along the length of the piece; cupping a hollow across the width of a board; and twist where the corners of a board spiral so they are not in the same plane.

# *Index*

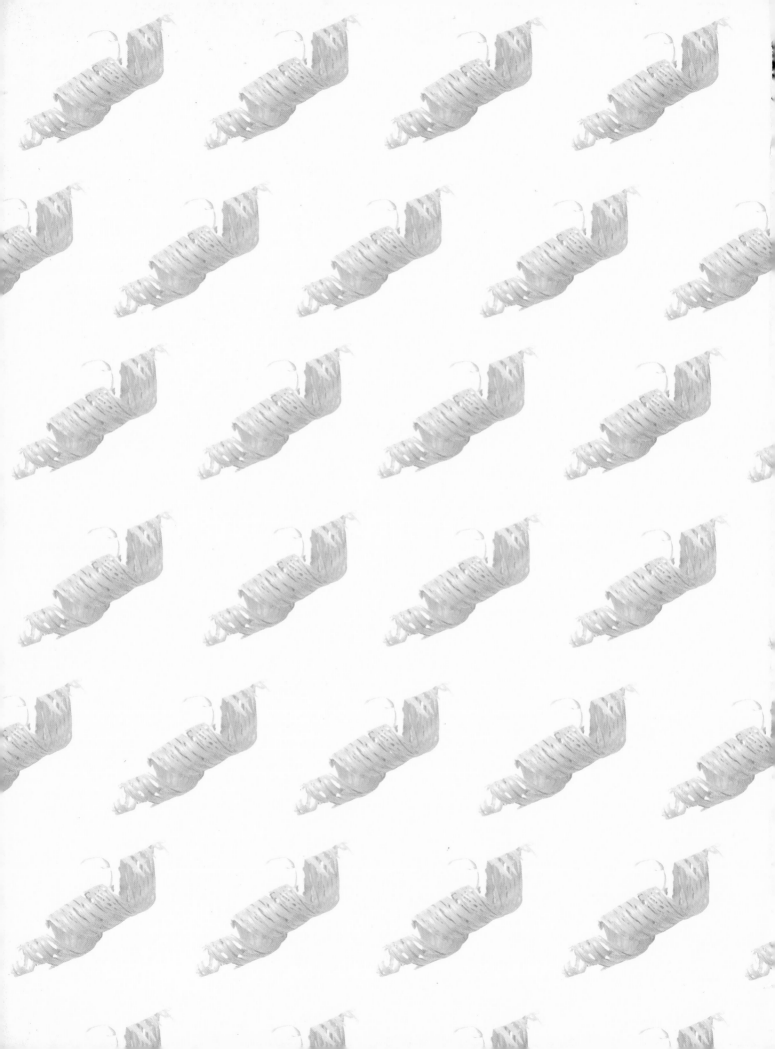